Gender
and
Anthropology

Gender
and
Anthropology

Frances E. Mascia-Lees
Simon's Rock College of Bard

Nancy Johnson Black
Metropolitan State University

WAVELAND
PRESS, INC.
Long Grove, Illinois

For information about this book, contact:
Waveland Press, Inc.
4180 IL Route 83, Suite 101
Long Grove, IL 60047-9580
(847) 634-0081
info@waveland.com
www.waveland.com

14

For my husband, Francis C. Lees
and
my sister, Marie Mascia-Rand

With love and gratitude for taking such good care of me.

FEM-L

For Thomas A. Weist
and
Hillary Marin Weeks

For showing me how important balance is in one's life,
and for keeping me on my toes.

NJB

Contents

Preface

AIMS AND LIMITATIONS

Our aim in this book is to outline in broad strokes the wide range of approaches that have been used over the last century by anthropologists interested in studying and understanding gender. In an introductory book of this limited size, it is impossible to cover the full range of topics, authors, and studies that have contributed to the field of gender studies in anthropology. In making choices about what to include in our coverage of the field, we have tried to balance breadth and depth. We are all too aware, however, of the many places where this goal has led us to move more quickly than we would have liked over the complexities, ambiguities, and nuances of certain ideas and issues or where we have had to exclude discussion of an influential study or author.

While we have tried to present a wide spectrum of ideas and approaches, our conceptualization of the study of gender in anthropology should not be taken as definitive. Just as gender is dynamic, so too is the field of gender studies where definitions, approaches, and commitments are highly controversial and actively contested (see Hirsch and Fox Keller 1990 for a review of many of these debates). Similarly, just as gender is an emotionally charged topic in North American society, so too is it within the field of anthropology where attention or inattention to gender and other forms of social difference have concrete and serious consequences for people's lives.

GENDER TERMINOLOGY USED IN THIS BOOK

There are a number of terms that are used throughout this book with which students need to be familiar. *Gender roles* or *gender behaviors* are the social skills, abilities, and ways of acting thought appropriate to members of a society depending upon whether they are male or female. Anthropologists are particularly interested in uncovering the reasons for the differences in the roles assigned to men and women as well as in the relationship of these roles to the differential access men and women have to power and authority in their society.

Sexual status is the position each sex occupies in relation to the other. Understanding what constitutes a person's position or status is a complicated issue for anthropologists interested in cross-cultural comparisons. The difficulty arises because what determines a person's status is not consistent across cultures. We cannot, therefore, use Western ideas about what high status means and simply apply them to another society, assuming that the basis for determining women's position is the same everywhere. For example, while people in the United States might see a woman's right to compete equally with men for access to any occupation as a sign of high status, being able to do men's work in another society might have little or even negative significance for determining a woman's position. Whether this access affects women's status would depend on a large number of other factors, including whether a higher value was placed on men's work or whether women's exclusion resulted in their unequal access to their society's resources or privileges.

Sexual or *gender stratification* is the system of unequal access of men and women to a society's resources, privileges, and opportunities, and the differential control over these resources and privileges accorded by sex. This hierarchical system reflects the expectations of a particular society or subculture. It arises from a group's differential evaluation of males and females and their roles, and the status they are allotted based on that assessment. *Gender asymmetry* refers to the situation in which men's and women's roles are not the same and their positions in society are not equal.

GOALS OF THE BOOK

Our multiple commitments and concerns have led us to address the following goals in this book. First, we want to introduce students to how anthropologists using different theoretical orientations have approached the study of gender roles and gender inequality. We begin with the late nineteenth century, the moment when anthropology emerged as a distinct academic discipline, and end with some of the newest approaches being offered in the field today. By placing these approaches in historical perspective, we show how anthropological approaches to studying women and men, gender roles, and gender inequality have changed over time in relation to changing social and political contexts. In providing this historical contextualization, we do not mean to imply that there has been a simple linear progression in anthropological studies of gender from older, less adequate theories, ideas, and approaches to newer, better ones. To depict the anthropological study of gender in this way would be to gloss over a more complex reality. As Micaela di Leonardo asserts, behind any facade of progress in anthropological studies of gender is "a complex history of roads traveled and then abandoned, new starts and alliances and fissures across disciplines and among anthropological subfields" (1991:1).

Our second concern is to provide students with techniques of analysis that will help them make their own critical assessments of studies of gender. We hope to show the usefulness of understanding the underlying tenets of different theoretical approaches to studying gender and sexual inequality, and how using anthropological data from around the world allows researchers to question unproven assumptions about these factors. Thus, we have organized the chapters in this book according to the primary theoretical orientations that have been used in anthropology to investigate gender: the evolutionary, psychological, materialist, ideational, discourse, sociolinguistic, and reflexive orientations. We are aware that many ideas do not fit into these theoretical orientations as neatly as we have made them appear, but we have chosen to privilege our desire for clarity over our awareness of complexity. Our main concern is to make clear the basic assumptions and goals of various theoretical orientations and to assess the validity of any particular theory by the extent to which it can be supported with evidence.

Lastly, we hope that these analytical efforts will help students in their own attempts to understand gender and the role it plays in their own lives. Toward this end, we have included in chapter 1 our own personal statements about the impact gender ideologies have had on us in both our personal and professional lives.

Acknowledgments

We would like to thank Dr. Frederick T. Kirchhoff, Dean of the College of Arts and Sciences at Metropolitan State University for his support, which greatly facilitated our collaboration on this book. We would also like to acknowledge the importance of Louise Lamphere's work to our thinking, and the help she has so graciously provided over the years. Family members and friends have offered invaluable assistance. We wish to thank them for it, especially Francis C. Lees for keeping us warm and well fed while we worked, Alexander Lees for his helpful feedback, Tom Weist and Laura Merilatt for their assistance, and Monte Bute for sharing his library. Thanks also to Joan del Plato, Pat Sharpe, and Barbara Resnik for their help with suggesting book cover ideas.

We would also like to thank Naomi Quinn and MaryCarol Hopkins who, in reviewing the manuscript, provided us with excellent recommendations for making it stronger. We do regret, however, that due to space limitations, we were unable to take all of their suggestions. Despite all the helpful feedback we have received, we bear all responsibility for the views expressed in this work.

Chapter One

The History
of the Study of Gender
in Anthropology

GENDER AS A CULTURAL CONSTRUCT

If you were born a male instead of a female, or a female instead of a male, how would your life be different? In other words, how has your sex defined, constructed, constrained, or expanded your opportunities and experiences? This question is essentially about gender, since gender can be understood as the meanings that a particular society gives to the physical or biological traits that differentiate males and females. These meanings provide members of a society with ideas about how to act, what to believe, and how to make sense of their experiences. The significance of these interpretations can have major consequences for individuals. In some societies, it can mean the difference between happiness and misery and, in others, even between life and death.

The discipline of anthropology is well suited to investigating this kind of variation. Anthropologists compare the similarities and differences found in various societies, and look for explanations of them. When differences are uncovered, anthropologists are able to call into question claims made about the universality of human behavior. When similarities are found, anthropologists attempt to uncover the factor or factors shared among various human groups that might best explain commonalities. Explaining variation in gender roles has been the particular concern of feminist anthropology. As we will see, this field has made important contributions to assessing the validity of notions prev-

1

alent in the United States and other Western societies about the supposed inherent differences between men and women.

In North American (the United States and Canada) society, meanings are assigned to males and females at the moment of birth. When a child is born, among the first questions asked is, "Is it a boy or a girl?" With the increased use of amniocentesis, many parents now routinely want to know the sex of their child before birth so they can make appropriate plans. Advances in selective spermicide may soon allow parents to determine the sex of their baby before conception, an option desired by 40 percent of respondents in a recently televised poll. While we might be less concerned today than we were in the past with dressing a baby boy in blue and a baby girl in pink, a child's sex continues to be significant for how parents think about and treat their children.

The largely unconscious process of training girls to be women and boys to be men is still central to a child's socialization in contemporary societies, even though in many Western societies expectations have changed and widened in the last few decades. Videotaped research of parents with their newborn infants, for example, reveals that parents think of their babies in stereotypic ways. Sons are more often described as strong, healthy, and alert, and daughters are characterized as soft, delicate, and passive. These characterizations occur despite evidence that males are more vulnerable physically than females, dying at a higher rate than females at all ages, except during a woman's childbearing years. Culture constructs definitions of masculinity and femininity that have consequences for how each of us is treated in innumerable ways during our lifetime.

Yet since gender constructs are cultural interpretations of physical differences, they are open to change. This dynamic aspect of culture is not surprising because culture, as anthropologists define it, is a system of meaning that is *learned* and shared by members of a group. Culture organizes people's behavior and thoughts in the context of their society's history and environment. Since individuals learn cultural ideas within the context of their society, gender constructs and expectations can be unlearned and modified, although the process can be quite difficult.

THE NATURE/NURTURE CONTROVERSY

Defining gender as a cultural construct suggests that gender is largely due to nurture or cultural practices and ideas, not to "nature" or biological causes. This nurture position is, however, somewhat controversial in everyday North American society and also within some academic fields because of the widespread belief that gender behaviors are inborn.

When you hear clichés like "boys will be boys" or "she does that just like a woman," the assumption is usually that gender behaviors are the result of innate causes, not the result of cultural interpretations that are learned by members of a society. Similarly, when scientific articles purport that there is a genetic basis for men's infidelity or for women "playing hard to get" in the dating game, they, too, are claiming that gendered behaviors are natural, not cultural. But which are they? And how would you go about deciding, rather than merely accepting, whether a behavior or characteristic is inborn or learned or whether it is the result of some combination of the two?

These questions are important because of the tendency in many Western societies to equate what is thought to be inborn and natural with what is right and unchangeable. Moreover, supposed natural differences between the sexes have been used historically to rationalize and further systems of oppression and even to determine social policy. For example, toward the end of the nineteenth century it was erroneously concluded that men were naturally superior to women in intelligence because of the larger size of their brains. This assumption was used to rationalize women's exclusion from higher education. We know now that variation in human brain size is not related to intelligence and that men and women as groups do not differ on measures of intelligence.

Today, it is not brain size but the way men and women use their brains that supposedly explains gender differences in capabilities and behavior. For instance, men and women are repeatedly studied to discern whether they use the left or right hemisphere of the brain for certain functions. However, conclusions based on these brain lateralization and function studies are often as faulty as those of the craniologists who measured people's skulls to determine intelligence a hundred years ago. For example, in a recent article on the findings of contemporary brain research, Diane Hales (1998) reports that new brain-imaging techniques reveal that neurons fire all over a woman's brain when she puts her mind to work. In contrast, in men's brains, neurons fire in highly specific areas. Admitting that "we don't yet know the implications of these findings" (p. 128), Hales nevertheless links this neurological variation to men's supposed superior ability to concentrate. She then concludes that this difference in brain functioning may explain why "husbands can immerse themselves in the sports page while the baby cries, the phone rings, and the dog barks" (p. 173). But do men really concentrate better than women? The evidence is questionable. Furthermore, brain researchers admit that they do not know what the gender differences in neural firing in the brain mean. Thus the conclusion that the pattern in men's brains explains why they supposedly don't get up from reading about football or hockey to comfort their crying children is obviously an unwarranted and erroneous one, arrived at by making enormous logical leaps. Nonetheless, conclusions like these are repeatedly reported in the press and lend credence to the popular belief that biology holds the key to understanding men and women.

Human behavior almost certainly has both a biological and a social basis, but the relative influence of these two factors is extremely difficult to discern, despite new sophisticated technologies for isolating genes or for observing brain activity. Contrary to what many researchers in the natural and social sciences claim, the data that would allow them to demonstrate that a gendered behavior is unquestionably biologically determined, whether by hormones, genes, or differences in brain structure, do not exist today. Scientists are putting forth hypotheses and theories that are open to question.

Claims about the inherent basis of men's and women's behavior should indeed be questioned because it has been shown repeatedly that researchers employ biases and assumptions without recognizing them, giving rise to conclusions that are often more ideological than scientific. If you have any doubt that scientific arguments like these need to be questioned, perhaps the recent claim made by Professor Dennis K. McBride, a political scientist at George Mason University—that there is a genetic basis for the propensity of liberal politicians to wear beards— might prompt you to change your mind (*Chronicle of Higher Education*, 1998).

Such biological determinist arguments, whether about liberals and conservatives or men and women, greatly oversimplify the complex set of factors that influence human behaviors. Nonetheless, many people are eager to accept them because simple explanations offer a certainty that makes negotiating our complex world seem easier. Acceptance of untested assumptions about gender is particularly appealing today because of the confusing and contradictory messages about gender with which the media bombard us daily. Are women sex objects or competent members of the workplace? One reason it is hard to decide is because toy stores carry Barbie Dolls dressed as airplane pilots, even though less than 5 percent of actual commercial pilots were women as of 1996. Are men macho or nurturing? It is difficult to tell. John Gray's best-selling book, *Men Are from Mars, Women Are from Venus* (1992), underscores men's supposed competitive, self-centered tendencies. At the same time, situation comedies like *Mad About You* portray husbands as caring and equal partners with their wives in child rearing and household chores.

Such contradictory messages have led to significant confusion about how one is expected to behave. This role ambiguity may be encountered in a number of social situations ranging from the trivial to the significant; it may, for example, make men hesitant to hold a door open for a woman, or it might deter a woman from entering higher-paying, male-dominated fields, such as construction work or engineering.

ROOTS OF THE NORTH AMERICAN WOMEN'S MOVEMENT

While contradictory messages are a source of confusion today, narrow gender expectations were the rule well into the 1970s. During those times, the roles assigned to men and women in North American society were restricted in comparison to those that are available today. At the time, it was typical to define men almost exclusively by their roles as breadwinners and leaders, that is, by their activities outside the home in the socially valued spheres of business and politics. In contrast, women were expected to remain at home and to be satisfied by their roles as housewives and mothers, even though this option was open to only a limited number of women who actually could afford to do so. Women who had no choice but to enter the labor force were unable to attain this cultural ideal of the female role. Consequently, they were seen as inferior, as inadequate, and as less feminine and desirable than other women.

These rigid gender expectations went largely unquestioned because almost every segment of North American society seemed to conform to them, making them appear natural and normal. On television, the *Ozzie and Harriet Show* provided a picture of the ideal North American family, one composed of a hard-working father and a homemaker mother who had freshly baked cookies ready for her sons when they came home from school. From the pulpit, clergy such as the Reverend Billy Graham preached the sanctity of a wife's obedience to her husband. In Washington, D.C., an almost all-male Congress passed laws for the entire U.S. population while military bases housed a fighting force made up of men ready to ensure the safety of democracy at the height of the cold war. On the campuses of elite higher educational institutions in the United States, many privileged women sought not an advanced education, but a "Mrs." degree.

For many women, especially women of color and women from working-class backgrounds, earning the Mrs. degree was not an option, and any aspiration they might have toward a higher education was seen as misplaced and impractical. Women who felt dissatisfied with the limitations such restrictive expectations imposed were frequently labeled neurotic or abnormal, and magazine articles at the time even cautioned them that a college degree might make finding a husband more difficult (Martin 1987:186). The pressure for women to eschew education in favor of finding a husband is clearly evident in the following personal recollection by Nancy Black:

> When I entered Flushing High School in 1961, my firefighter father and homemaker mother informed me that they could only afford to send one of their four children to college—and the chosen one would be their only son, my younger brother by 6 years. They stood firm in their decision, insisting I take commercial courses in high school, including stenography, typing, and bookkeeping. They weren't even that invested in my high school education: before my commencement, my mother asked me if I minded if she and my father not attend my high school graduation ceremony. They had gone to my older sister's the year before, and since mine was to be held in the same RKO Keith's movie theater, they didn't see the point of sitting through a commencement again.
>
> So it is no surprise that my parents refused to pay the $6 fee for me to take the Scholastic Aptitude Test and opposed any discussion of my attending the almost tuition-free New York City college system, even though in 1964, tuition and fees totaled $24 a semester at Hunter College. So I used my baby-sitting money to pay for a one-time shot at the SATs, defused my parents' hostility by taking all the commercial courses my high school offered as well as its advanced academic courses, which would make me admissible to college. Despite my parents' objections, I applied to and was accepted at Hunter College. The first day of class at Hunter was the first time I set foot on a college campus. I could tell my parents thought I had made the wrong decision and that I was wasting my time, because their expectation was that I would soon marry and have children.

THE WOMEN'S MOVEMENT
AND THE STUDY OF GENDER

It was this social environment of limited expectations for women that Betty Friedan analyzed in her 1963 best-selling book, *The Feminine Mystique*. Focusing primarily on white, middle-class women, Friedan uncovered a pervasive discontent among them, a malaise that books and magazines told them was attributable to their own personal shortcomings. Friedan, by contrast, identified narrow societal definitions of gender roles that confined women to the home as the reason behind many women's dissatisfaction. *The Feminine Mystique*, along with the example set by civil rights activists and others demonstrating against U.S. social policies, was influential in sparking many women's awareness of inequality. Such factors provided a catalyst for women to protest their disenfranchisement from the resources and privileges of a largely male-dominated public sphere. With this recognition of women's oppression, the second wave of the women's movement began to form in the United States (the first wave had occurred around the turn of the twentieth century and ultimately led to granting women the right to vote). With it was unleashed a political force that had broad reverberations throughout North American society. Over the next few decades, almost every aspect of North American society was questioned in terms of its assumptions about the biological differences between men and women that restricted women's opportunities, and more and more women began to fight against the social injustices that plagued their lives. Contrary to today's popular belief, the women's movement was not a fringe group of a few vocal and radical troublemakers. Because women were undercompensated in the economy and overworked at home, millions of North Americans supported efforts to improve women's economic and social conditions.

A scrutiny of unproven assumptions about the cause of women's inequality, a central concern of the women's movement, also extended to many academic fields. For the first time, disciplines such as anthropology, sociology, and history, which traditionally had ignored the importance of gender, began to recognize the inattention given women in traditional social science investigations. Such inattention was particularly ironic in anthropology given its goal of understanding humans, not just men, within the context of their culture. Until the advent of feminism, anthropology largely treated women as invisible and ignored issues of gender (McGee and Warms 1996:392), as the following personal reflection by Fran Mascia-Lees suggests:

> I hadn't gone straight from high school to college, unsure of what I wanted to study anyway. Nonetheless, I found myself on college campuses where students protested the Vietnam War and other government initiatives. It was the early 1970s, and being at a peace moratorium at Yale, or at a demonstration against the U.S. invasion of Cambodia on the Ohio State campus, which ended with students getting tear gassed, was exhilarating. Anti-war protests offered a route to societal change like nothing I thought I could get in a stuffy classroom—until, that is, I casually glanced through a textbook sitting in the back seat of a friend's car as I waited for her to come out of the store with our M&Ms and Cokes.

> The small section I read in that book offered a vision of an alternative way to think about who I was or could become. It described societies that established important kinship relationships through links among women, a system of reckoning descent known as matrilineality. To me, a young woman who had been raised in a traditional household where boys were valued over girls, it was a revelation. Discovering a society that put women at the center fired my imagination; it allowed me to envision a world in which women mattered

in significant ways. I had serendipitously discovered anthropology. When the next semester began, I was enrolled in college, eager to find other societal models that might call into question the inevitability of the gender expectations I found so limiting.

Unfortunately, as I was to find out, the focus on women in matrilineal descent systems was actually one of the few places in which gender was considered important in anthropology at the time. Indeed, I discovered that many anthropologists erroneously projected what they saw as women's relative unimportance in Western societies on to non-Western societies, leading them to overlook the important contributions actually made by women in other societies. It wasn't until I was in graduate school that the promise I thought anthropology held for me years earlier was actually fulfilled. Two influential books, *Woman, Culture, & Society* (Rosaldo and Lamphere 1974) and *Toward an Anthropology of Women* (Reiter 1975a), came to my attention and ignited my intellectual interest once again.

THE RISE OF FEMINIST ANTHROPOLOGY

Many people have gravitated to anthropology over the years for the alternative societal models it offers. Through comparing practices in many different societies, anthropologists have demonstrated repeatedly how aspects of a particular society that are assumed to be universal and natural are really specific to it. When similar insights about gender roles and inequality emerged in the 1970s due to influences from the women's movement, the subdiscipline of feminist anthropology was born. It arose as a special subfield within anthropology, one committed to understanding systems of gender oppression, to analyzing forces of exclusion, and to working for social change.

Reclaiming Foremothers

Anthropological work that today we would call "feminist" had been done before the 1970s, but it had not been recognized as central to the discipline. Women anthropologists, such as Elsie Clews Parsons, Alice Fletcher, and Phyllis Kaberry, working in the first half of the twentieth century, wrote ethnographies forefronting women's voices, and Zora Neale Hurston, a black anthropologist and novelist, focused not just on women but on African-American men as well. Perhaps the best known of these early pioneers was Margaret Mead, who popularized anthropology and made significant contributions to the study of gender. She was one of the first to debunk simplistic claims about the biological causes of sex differences with such ethnographies as *Coming of Age in Samoa* (1928) and *Sex and Temperament in Three Primitive Societies* (1935).

However, while the work of these women was well regarded by many of their colleagues, it was not considered central to anthropology until feminist anthropologists of the 1970s established gender as pivotal to anthropological concerns and reclaimed the writing of these "foremothers" as significant. This work of reclamation remains an important part of feminist anthropology as recent articles on Elsie Clews Parsons (Lamphere 1995), Ruth Benedict (Babcock 1995), Ella Cara Deloria and Morning Dove (Finn 1995), Zora Neale Hurston (Hernández 1995), Ruth Landes (Cole 1995), Barbara Myerhoff (Frank 1995), and Margaret Mead (Lutkehaus 1995) indicate.

Questioning Assumptions

Feminist anthropologists not only approached the work of these pioneering women anthropologists in new ways; they also looked at many different societies, past and present, with fresh eyes. In doing so, they began to uncover a wide range of variation in gender roles, in the value placed on activities performed by men and women, and in men's and women's access to important societal resources. They began to question the assumptions about gender differences that underpinned women's social inequality in their own society. If Mende women in Africa could be long-distance traders, feminist anthropologists asked, then wasn't the assumption in Western societies of the naturalness of women's position as stay-at-home caretakers subject to question? If Ju/'hoansi women of the Kalahari Desert were the primary "breadwinners" in their society and Ojibwe women of the Great Lakes region of North America active warriors, then wasn't it possible that cultural assumptions, not biologically inherent causes, might explain women's supposed inability to contribute to the economic and political spheres in Western societies?

The early phase of feminist anthropology produced a wide range of studies that concentrated on identifying what women's position, or status, was cross-culturally. Concerned with the view of women produced by traditional anthropology, feminist anthropologists exposed biases in earlier anthropological studies and exposed how male-centered, or androcentric, perspectives had helped create a distorted picture, one that seriously underestimated the importance of women's work and place in society. In the past, the majority of ethnographies were written by males, or by females trained by males, who collected information largely from and about men in other societies. Anthropologist Alice Schlegel, remarking about the consequences of this situation noted that

> one gets the impression from many ethnographers that culture is created by and for men between the ages of puberty and late middle age, with children, women, and the aged as residual categories; women are frequently portrayed, at best, as providing support for the activities of men. (1977:2)

Such data were frequently presented as the reality of a society rather than as representing only part of the cultural whole. This kind of bias was not specific to anthropology. Psychologist Carol Gilligan, for example, revealed in her groundbreaking study, *In a Different Voice* (1982), that the widespread conclusion that women are less morally developed than men was based on analyses that used men as the norm and failed to include women as research subjects. Using men as the standard and excluding women from experiments also routinely occurred in medical studies, often having devastating consequences for women.

Feminist anthropologists used the new cross-cultural data they were producing not only to correct the ethnographic record but also to question biological determinist accounts of gender. They argued that variation in the roles and status of men and women uncovered by their studies suggested that gender might not be determined by biology.

Variation in Approaches to Gender Analysis

The focus on gender as a cultural construct rather than as a biological certainty did not mean, however, that there was agreement among all feminist anthropologists about how best to conceptualize and understand gender roles and inequality. Differences among researchers during this early phase of feminist anthropology served to enrich our understanding of women's roles and position. Numerous ethnographies were written, providing rich documentation of the role gender plays in societies around the world (see, for example, Bell 1983; Bledsoe 1980; Caplan 1985; Goodale [1971] 1994; Moore 1986; Murphy and Murphy 1974; Shostak 1983; Strathern 1972; Weiner 1979; Wolf 1972). Despite differences among researchers, early feminist anthropologists did agree on one thing: that it was essential to take gender into account when attempting to understand how a society operates or how an individual's identity and life experiences are shaped.

This commitment to gender as a category of analysis has been complicated somewhat by more recent studies in feminist anthropology. Gender is now understood as only one factor affecting people's lives. Other kinds of "difference," such as race, class, ethnicity, sexual preference, and physical ability, are studied for the way they interact with gender to produce different degrees of privilege and experiences of oppression for different groups of people. Feminist anthropologists who study "the politics of difference" have not confined their analyses to women either. Their commitment to uncovering and fighting social injustice and inequality has led them to investigate the lives of oppressed men around the world as well.

CONCLUSIONS

This book discusses the major trends in feminist anthropology and provides an overview of its development from the 1970s, the period in which we ourselves first began to question and realize how gender, and other markers of difference, operated within our own lives. As we were growing up, we were initially largely unaware of how society's gender and class norms imposed limitations on us. It took a burgeoning women's movement to help us articulate and make sense out of our dissatisfactions with the constraints on our lives. This process of understanding how societal definitions limited the very ideas we had about who we were, or could become, was a long and arduous one.

As we suggested earlier, today the situation is in many ways even more complex. On the one hand, many scholarly books and articles seem obsessed with convincing us that gender roles and behaviors are limited, innate, and inevitable. On the other hand, popular culture suggests that gender does not really restrict one's choices and sense of self. Indeed, contradictory messages from the media imply that individuals can have it all. They suggest that each of us can be anything we wish, if, that is, we buy the right products or work hard enough. Yet in many societies, significant discrepancies exist between men's and women's access to opportunities and in the quality of their lives. In the United States, for example, women and children continue to comprise the majority of people living below the poverty level; women's wages continue to lag behind men's for comparable work; women continue to hit a "glass ceiling" that constrains their opportunities for advancement in their careers; women are more likely than men to experience the double burden of working outside the home while simultaneously having responsibility for work in the home; and women continue to be physically battered by boyfriends and husbands at an alarming rate. Such patterns are typical of the disparities between men and women in many contemporary Western societies.

If biological determinist arguments are to be believed, these patterns are due to innate differences between men and women and are thus inevitable. If popular culture is right—that we can all be anything we choose—then the undesirable circumstances in which women find themselves must be their own fault. Neither of these explanations, however, takes sufficient account of the complexity of human culture and of the factors affecting human behavior.

Anthropology, by contrast, is interested in just such complexities and in explaining the intricacies of human culture and behavior, even if these explanations don't support fashionable, but untested, assumptions about gender differences or offer the most interesting sound bites for the evening news. By revealing how gender operates in non-Western societies, anthropology provides information that can be used to assess theoretical claims made about men and women in Western societies. This knowledge can act as a background against which to examine your own experiences. Our hope is that the anthropological approaches in this book will provide you with some new insights into the role gender plays in your life, knowledge that may aid you in dealing with societal forces that might limit your opportunities and choices.

Chapter Two

Analyzing Theories

Each of us is a theoretician: we all have ideas about how the world works and why humans behave the way they do, ideas that guide our daily actions. These everyday or folk theories are often greatly influenced by theories derived from the natural and social sciences. What differentiates the two types of theories, however, is that the second type exists as part of a self-conscious, systematic, and formally organized body of knowledge known as a theoretical orientation.

We begin this chapter with an exploration of the effects of differing theoretical orientations on conclusions reached by researchers investigating gender. We then outline some of the important dimensions of analysis used by various researchers. These dimensions crosscut theoretical orientations. Therefore, knowledge about how they operate should help you in your own analyses of the different conclusions reached by researchers, regardless of the particular theoretical orientation they use.

THEORETICAL ORIENTATIONS

Theoretical orientations are based on a set of assumptions and accepted principles that provide a broad frame of reference for researchers and a general context for their investigations. Theoretical orientations guide researchers in choosing a subject, conceptualizing a problem, framing questions, investigating a topic, and interpreting and presenting results. Therefore, theoretical orientations profoundly influence the conclusions reached about a topic. Compare, for example, the conclusions about male aggression arrived at by investigators using the different theoretical orientations described below.

Many *biosocial* investigators have theorized that men are naturally more aggressive than women. The theoretical orientation within which they work assumes that complex human behaviors can be explained through the principle of natural selection: that individuals with traits best suited to particular environmental conditions are more likely to survive and pass on their genes to subsequent generations. This premise has led them to investigate the similarities between male aggression in humans and in nonhuman animals. They argue that if male aggression is found in many animal species, it must have played an important part in survival. Finding some such similarities, biosocial investigators conclude that male aggression has a biological basis, one that has been selected for in the course of evolution. Assuming females play little or no role in mate choice, they hypothesize that aggressive males win out over their rivals in the competition for mates, thereby passing on their own genes, including the ones that code for aggression. But are these assumptions, forms of investigation, and conclusions the only viable ones?

Social learning theorists begin from the opposite premise from biosocial investigators. They argue that biological explanations cannot account for the high degree of variation found in male aggressiveness in societies around the world. If men are more aggressive than women, proponents of this theoretical orientation argue, it is because in some societies boys learn to be aggressive from a very early age. They focus on how children learn gender role behaviors and argue that male aggression, like other human behaviors, is acquired through a process of socialization that prepares children for their adult roles. Parents, educators, peers, and popular culture all reinforce what they see as proper gender behaviors for boys and girls, leading children to imitate those of the appropriate sex, thriving on the rewards they get for doing so. Social learning theorists argue that if boys are aggressive it is because this behavior is validated, even encouraged, through both obvious and subtle mechanisms. Rather than compare male aggression across animal species, social learning theorists compare across and within human societies. They attempt to correlate variation in male aggressiveness with other social and cultural factors. For example, anthropologists Marvin and Carol Ember (1998:14) have found that higher levels of aggression are found in societies that approve of or glorify violence, whether in war, sports, the movies, or on television.

You might ask, "Well, which is the right theory?" This confusion arises because in everyday life when we hear the word "theory," we tend to think of ideas that are unproven. When a remark is made that we think is not based on "fact," many people dismiss its merits, saying "that's just a theory." But in the social sciences, theories are not "right" or "wrong"; they are either more or less well substantiated by the evidence or more or less useful in explaining a phenomenon or behavior.

Knowing the theoretical orientation out of which any particular knowledge arises is an important first step in analyzing it. However, other dimensions of analysis crosscut theoretical orientations. For example, a researcher may assume that women are universally subordinate to men whether employing a biosocial or social learning orientation. Researchers using the same theoretical orientation may differ according to whether they see "woman" as a useful category of analysis, whether they recognize the limitations of this unitary construct and choose instead to focus on the intersection of gender with other markers of difference such as race and class.

CHALLENGING ESSENTIALISM

We have made the point that one dimension along which theories of gender and sexual stratification differ is whether priority is given to biological or cultural factors in different accounts, but this nature versus nurture controversy is only one area of contention that has beset gender studies.

Another area of disagreement concerns whether all women share certain experiences because of biological similarities. The claim that they do is known as *essentialism*. As we have seen, feminists have accused biosocial theorists of essentializing gender, that is, of understanding gender as a fundamental entity based in biology. But some feminists, too, have been accused of essentializing when they use the category "woman" (see de Lauretis 1990 for an overview of this debate). Narrowly conceived definitions of woman, critics claim, have failed to consider how other factors such as class, race, ethnicity, religion, sexual preference, and physical ability intersect with gender to produce widely different experiences for women. Theories that assume that women can be treated as a single, unified category have often been challenged by ones that take into account how other systems of oppression intersect with gender discrimination, differentially excluding and burdening women who come from different backgrounds (see, for example, Lugones and Spelman 1983; Mohanty, Russo, and Torres 1991).

VARIATION OR UNIVERSAL SUBORDINATION?

Theories of status vary according to whether women are assumed to have a lower position than men do in all societies, thereby rendering them universally subordinate (see, for example, Rosaldo 1974). Those who argue that women are not universally subordinate to men point to the variation in women's status around the world (see, for example, Reiter 1975b). These researchers tend to compare different societies, some in which women's position is high and others in which it is low, hoping to isolate those factors that can account for this difference.

Theorists who claim that women are universally subordinate are making an assumption that is almost impossible to verify. For even if every known society places women in a secondary position to men in every realm (and this is not necessarily the case), that does not mean there has never been a truly egalitarian society. One may have existed long ago before its gender system was documented or before Western gender notions were exported around the world through colonialism and global capitalism. Nonetheless, there are theorists who argue that since there is no known society in which women are superior to men and there are many in which they are not, it is appropriate to view women as universally the "second sex." They account for variation in women's experiences by pointing out that while women have been oppressed as a class, differences within gender are also used to subordinate women differentially. Researchers who adopt this position argue that

> when men deny women rights, the category woman applies to all who are clearly embodied female, but when men offer privileges, the very entitlements that appear to be rooted in female anatomy can be shown to emerge from the grounds of race and class, heterosexual orientation and physical ability. (Conboy, Medina, and Stanbury 1997:5)

Researchers who claim that women everywhere are subordinate to men search for the factor all societies have in common that might explain this position.

NEGOTIATION AND RESISTANCE

Many traditional anthropological accounts tend to focus on societies as static or unchanging. Some feminist anthropologists have contested this approach because it fails to recognize that both men and women make choices and act within their societies in ways that can influence change. This *interactionist*, or "practice," approach focuses on how people, as the active interpreters of symbolic gender meanings, may work within the constraints imposed by their societies. In some of the earliest interactionist studies, feminist anthropologists examined women's actions in societies that excluded them from official decision making, and found that women often maximized their interests and gains privately by influencing the decisions of their husbands and sons (Collier 1974) or by creating alliances with women from other households, manipulating opinions through informal discussion (Lamphere 1974).

More recent work of this type has focused on how different groups of women in the United States negotiate and contest the way society constructs the categories of male and female and the meanings associated with them (see Ginsburg and Tsing 1990:2). A study by Kathleen Stewart (1990), for example, reveals that Appalachian women use an argumentative dialogue and storytelling to contest dominant definitions of gender and to produce a world in which they can "speak for themselves." Other recent studies focus on more overt forms of women's political activism, such as the social organizations women form in Belize to resist and challenge male dominance (McClaurin 1996).

Arguing that systems of oppression are never all-encompassing, interactionist studies like these are interested in how people act upon, negotiate, and resist the social categorizations that define and constrain them. Such investigations are often less interested in cross-cultural comparisons than in how categories of difference within any particular society are open to challenge and change.

POLITICAL CONTEXTS/ETHICAL CHOICES

Cultural Context

It is important to remember that we know of no laws of human behavior. Every idea put forth today to explain gender behavior is a hypothesis, and although some hypotheses are better substantiated by evidence than others, none is unquestioningly true. In other words, there is no purely objective explanation for the differences in behavior assumed to exist between men and women, despite claims to the contrary. Work in the social sciences is the consequence of scientific inquiry that has a social character. Just as our everyday folk beliefs about men and women are affected by scientific theories, so scientific theories about gender are themselves greatly influenced by the cultural milieu out of which they arise. Thus it is not surprising to find erroneous ideas shared by both scientific researchers and members of the public.

For example, there is a widespread notion in North American society that physiological differences between the sexes naturally fit men and women for particular roles. This position is readily apparent in the following statement by former Speaker of the House Newt Gingrich in a lecture to students on why women are not suited for traditional military combat and men are: "If combat means living in a ditch, females have biological problems staying in a ditch for 30 days because they get infections . . . males are biologically driven to go out and hunt giraffes" (*Newsweek* 1995:17). Because they share a cultural milieu, it is not surprising to find similarities in the assumptions underlying Gingrich's statement and those of biosocial researchers. Both assume that men today are better suited to hunting and fighting because they developed the physical abilities necessary for these activities through the process of evolution. Yet there is no direct evidence that, in our species' past, men were the hunters and warriors exclusively. Evidence from contemporary societies contradicts this claim too; in some societies women hunt, and in others they participate in warfare (Jones 1997).

The assumption that there is a natural relationship between physical attributes and gender roles often goes unquestioned in many contemporary Western societies. But not all societies assume this relationship. Among the Sambia of New Guinea, for example, boys become men of strength through a series of rites in which they orally "receive" the semen of adult males (Herdt 1982). It is this culturally produced strength that is seen to prepare young men for warfare, not some inborn ability or physical characteristic. The idea that men and women are produced through cultural rites is at the base of many rituals in non-Western societies. These kinds of rites of passage, or "initiation ceremonies," turn boys into men and girls into women. Such ceremonies also institute the proper societal relationship between the sexes which are thus seen as cultural, not natural. For example, among the Okiek of Kenya, girls are thought of as dependent children prior to undergoing a ritual process from which they emerge as women whose relationship with men will henceforth be one of interdependence (Kratz 1994).

Similarities or Differences?

The fact that researchers in many Western countries choose to focus on the differences between men and women, rather than similarities, is itself a product of the history and social and political agendas of these societies. This interest in difference is so deeply embedded in North American society that suggesting that gender similarities might be as significant and interesting an area of research as gender differences tends to strike most people as absurd. But, why? It is not impossible to imagine a context in which raising questions about differences in ethnic groups would seem equally ridiculous. Just think about the widespread view during the Nazi era that biological differences between Jews and non-Jews were great. Today, most people find claims that vast biological differences exist between groups of people to be unwarranted. The idea that biological factors best explain the differences between Jews and other cultural or religious groups strikes most people as ludicrous.

It is helpful to think about the degree of difference between males and females in another way. What if we were to use circles to depict gender differences in a Venn diagram, which is a drawing that represents sets and their relationships? We would have two circles, one representing men's behavior and another women's. It is readily apparent that the circles would overlap considerably. The places that did not overlap would represent the differences between the sexes and would constitute a rather small amount of each circle. Yet so much is made of this limited number of differences in the media that we start to believe that men and women easily could come from different planets, with Mars and Venus coming to mind. Moreover, millions of dollars each year are devoted to research that will help explain the behaviors or abilities that people assume fall into the non-overlapping areas of the circles. It should not be surprising that these traits are often ones that have important social consequences in terms of decisions about access to opportunities or resources.

Understanding the political context out of which ideas about gender arise, then, is crucial for making sense out of competing theories. But it is not always easy to figure out what motivates researchers to ask certain questions, or what political agenda their ideas serve. Feminist anthropologists, however, have been fairly forthright about their intentions. As we suggested in chapter 1, their concern is to articulate research interests with the goal of understanding and ending oppression. Many feminist anthropologists link theoretical knowledge with an active search for social change in society. This commitment means that they are particularly wary of arguments that serve conservative political agendas that maintain the status quo and its inequalities.

CONCLUSIONS

Because scientific research is so valued in contemporary society, it is often difficult to accept that it is affected by factors external to it. It is understandable, then, that people often resist questioning scientific "truths," especially when they are reinforced in the larger culture. But as any good scientist knows, hypotheses are meant to be scrutinized, and vigorously so. Our aim in the subsequent chapters is to do just that.

Chapter Three

The Evolutionary Orientation

While no one denies that men and women differ biologically, there is great variation in the importance placed on these differences by researchers interested in understanding gender roles and the existence of systems of sexual stratification. Anthropologists who have focused on biological differences and biosocial explanations have tended to employ evolutionary models in their explanations. Finding explanations of gender differences in evolutionary factors has a long history within anthropology, because the first school of anthropological theory, known as *social evolutionism*, used an evolutionary model to explain all aspects of human social organization.

By the early twentieth century, however, social evolutionism was largely in disrepute, abandoned because of its problematic assumptions about Western superiority and its claim that societies were like species that had evolved through a struggle for survival. The rejection of social evolutionism has not, however, meant that evolutionary explanations of gender have disappeared. To the contrary, these explanations are again quite popular today. While differences in societies are no longer attributed to how evolved they are, particular human behaviors, especially gender behaviors, are now routinely explained by how they have helped our species compete in its evolutionary struggle for survival.

This chapter traces the development of evolutionary thinking about gender from late nineteenth-century social evolutionism to contemporary explanations grounded in sociobiology and the closely related field of evolutionary psychology. It is hard to believe that social theories proposed in the nineteenth century are worthy of study today, but the degree of similarity in the underlying assumption between nineteenth- and twentieth-century evolutionary explanations is surprising. Current approaches focus on differential reproductive strategies in ways nineteenth-century thinkers did not. Nevertheless, like their nineteenth-century counterparts, contemporary theorists begin with the assumption that the gender roles that exist in their own societies are natural. Therefore, they seek explanations in the concepts of natural selection. As we will see, these contemporary thinkers are often just as interested as past researchers were in supporting prevailing gender arrangements, although the former focuses on the differences found between the sexes in the way they attract a mate, form bonds, or behave within marriage, not on the natural inferiority of women. Our intent in this chapter is to explain the popularity of these approaches by placing them in historical context and to assess the validity of the conclusions reached about gender roles and behavior through the use of evolutionary models.

SOCIAL EVOLUTIONISM

British and North American societies in the late nineteenth century were steeped in notions of progress and Western superiority. The West's progress, it was claimed, was due to its exceptional scientific technology and social advancements, which had enabled the success of its far-flung military and economic expansion. Indeed, Great Britain had such vast dominion over colonies throughout the world that one could rightfully remark that the sun never set on the British Empire. Colonialism was rationalized by systems of knowledge that supported the notion that conquered peoples were inherently inferior. One such system is still all too familiar to us today: it based assumptions of inferiority and superiority on the notion of race, "a cultural classification designed to deal with social problems, not a scientific classification in genetics . . ." (Bohannan 1992:183). This system claimed that the darker-skinned inhabitants of the world were naturally inferior to white, lighter-skinned populations. In the late nineteenth and early twentieth centuries, differences within British and North American society were also explained and rationalized by scientists through reference to biological attributes: members of the lower classes, women, criminals, and other societal "outcasts" were all viewed as inherently inferior to white men (see Gilman 1985). Thus they were thought to be rightfully excluded from their society's economic, political, and cultural resources and privileges.

Anthropology began to emerge as a distinct academic discipline during this time. It distinguished itself from other fields interested in human behavior and social organization by its focus on non-Western societies. By the mid-nineteenth century, an ever-increasing amount of information about non-Western societies collected by missionaries, colonial administrators, and travelers had found its way into Victorian society. Faced with evidence of the wide-ranging differences between non-Western societies and their own, as well as among different non-Western societies, early anthropologists thought they could uncover general laws about human behavior that would help them make sense of this variation. They thought they found such laws in the evolutionary principles so popular at the time. These social evolutionists argued that societies had evolved from the simple to the complex, the chaotic to the organized, and the homogeneous to the heterogeneous. These theorists were immersed in beliefs about the desirability of progress, and since simpler societies were seen as less advanced, it made sense to them to view non-Western societies as inferior (see, for example, Tylor 1871). These views took hold given their compatibility with pre-existing societal notions: evolution could be equated with the West's progress toward "superior" forms, and the natural struggle of the "fittest" for survival could be equated with military efforts resulting in colonial domination.

Social evolutionists claimed that societies evolved through a fierce struggle for survival in which a more fit society like their own had won out over less fit ones. They pointed to Western civilization's political, economic, and cultural dominance over the rest of the world as evidence that it was the fittest form of social organization and, thus, the most highly evolved (see, for example, Spencer 1884). They not only saw the social practices, customs, and institutions of non-Western societies as inferior and less evolved but also claimed that they represented earlier stages in Western society's evolution. Non-Western societies were used, in other words, as living examples of the West's "primitive" past, one that was left behind as it struggled for supremacy.

The most well-known evolutionary scheme employed by social evolutionists, such as the North American anthropologist Lewis Henry Morgan ([1877] 1985) utilized in his book *Ancient Society*, was one that classified and ranked societies according to whether they existed in a stage of Savagery, Barbarism, or Civilization. These designations were determined by the presence or absence of traits that were assumed to be most desirable, and, thus, most evolved. Societies that lacked the sophisticated technology that would allow them to produce their own food, for example, were at the bottom of the evolutionary scale, belonging to the stage that social evolutionists termed Savagery. Those people at the bottom of the socio-economic scale within the social evolutionists' own societies, such as the urban poor, were also classified as savages. Many social thinkers viewed them, like their non-Western counterparts, as degenerate, bestial, and morally and intellectually bankrupt (Stocking 1987:213).

Non-Western societies that had risen above such lowliness by producing their own food through the domestication of plants and animals but had not produced a phonetic alphabet were viewed as Barbarian. Not surprisingly, the Western society to which social evolutionists belonged was thought of as at the highest stage of social evolution, that of Civilization. It not only had an industrial base for food production and a system of writing but, according to social evolutionists, it also had a superior set of social institutions, which had enabled the development of these factors.

These institutions, according to the early social evolutionist Herbert Spencer (1884), involved superior forms of family and gender role organization that ensured male rights and male dominance. They included monogamy, a marriage practice allowing a person to have only one spouse at a time, and patrilineality, a system of reckoning descent by tracing genealogical connections through men.

Spencer hypothesized, even though there was no evidence to support his claim, that the earliest societies were promiscuous and lacked any institution to regulate sexuality. This situation meant that knowledge of paternity was obscured. Out of these chaotic conditions evolved societies that traced descent matrilineally, or through the female line, giving a mother's kinship group rights to her children. Since matrilineality established some rights over progeny, societies that instituted it were classified at a higher evolutionary level than promiscuous ones. Nonetheless, according to Spencer, matrilineal societies were inherently weak because men lacked control over women and paternal authority over children. By contrast, any society that regulated paternity through monogamy or institutionalized it through tracing descent through the male line would increase the chances of its existence. In other words, institutionalized paternity would lead to institutionalized male protection, ensuring the vitality and survival of the entire society. A society that favored monogamy and accentuated the male line would be able to conquer those that did not, thereby increasing its size and strength. In the process it would become more complex and evolve to a higher stage of development (Spencer 1884:611–31).

According to Spencer, freeing women from productive labor would also increase a society's chances for survival, since it would allow women to devote all of their time and energy to being "fit" mothers. Due to the increased capacity of its industrial system, Spencer argued, Victorian England was able to accomplish this goal. Equating his own society's ideal notion of womanhood with evolutionary progress, Spencer praised women's exclusion from the public realm. He argued that women's exclusion was the natural consequence of a long evolutionary process that selected those women dedicated to their duties in the domestic sphere. The inability of women of the working classes to attain this position was taken as evidence of their inherent inferiority.

This evolutionary explanation was also invoked to rationalize women's continued exclusion from the public realm. Many scientists at the time claimed that women had a limited amount of vital energy. To ensure that women had enough energy for their childbearing and child-rearing duties, it had to be channeled away from other functions, such as the development of higher mental abilities. The concentration of energy on reproductive functions was responsible for women's supposed inferior mental capabilities, causing women to lack "the power of abstract reasoning and the most abstract of emotions, the sentiment of justice" (Spencer 1884:374). Such inadequacies, which made women unsuited for important activities in the public realm, were seen as the natural outcome of the struggle for the survival of the fittest. Women's attempts at the time to advocate for equal rights, especially at the voting booths, were, therefore, discounted and their demands were viewed as unnatural and perilous. If women were subordinate to men in Western society, opponents of women's equality argued, it was because biological necessities rendered them physically and intellectually inferior. Male dominance was thus seen to have evolutionary origins grounded in the biological differences between the sexes, especially those related to women's reproductive functions.

THE FEMINIST CRITIQUE
OF SOCIAL EVOLUTIONISM

Uncovering the questionable assumptions underlying social evolutionism is not difficult from the vantage point of the late twentieth century. Most obvious is the problematic starting point of these analyses. Social evolutionists set out to explain what they already assumed: that Western society and its gender arrangements were the result of an evolutionary process that produced forms of social organization superior to all others. Such assumptions were, however, not questioned or tested but merely asserted.

Our suspicions of using claims of superiority to justify political domination, whether of one society over another or one social group over another within the same society, have deepened considerably in the post-Holocaust, post-Vietnam, post-feminist world in which we live. We have come to see how racism, rather than being an explanation of Western superiority, rationalized Western expansion and how assuming the inherent inferiority of women and members of other disenfranchised groups justified white male control of desirable resources. Similarly, we are no longer comfortable with the ethnocentric claim that Western society is unquestioningly superior to all others because of advanced technology. Today we are all too aware of the profoundly detrimental consequences technology can wreak. The potential impact of nuclear weapons or chemical warfare on humans and the disastrous effects of chemical wastes and other industrial products on the environment are now cause for alarm, not celebration. Today, in our efforts to improve the health and the quality of life of individuals in highly industrialized societies, many people increasingly turn back to the herbal cures, holistic healing, and the sustainable forms of agriculture associated with nonindustrialized societies.

Most social scientists no longer hold the belief that societies can be equated with biological organisms able to evolve through processes of adaptation. While it is clear that all societies change, there is no universal law governing the direction of that change. Instead anthropologists today seek explanations for societal change in complex historical and environmental factors. Thus, the conflation of evolution with a natural progression toward some ultimate state of perfection has completely lost its currency, as has the tendency to use extant non-Western societies as representative of some past moment in time. Non-Western societies are not remnants of some earlier time; they are not living fossils. Each has its own unique history.

FUNCTIONALIST EXPLANATIONS OF GENDER ROLES

By the beginning of the early twentieth century, the kinds of criticisms discussed above forced social evolutionism into the background. Social evolutionary explanations of human social organization were superseded by new theoretical orientations like *functionalism*, which was the dominant school of thought in British anthropology well into the twentieth century. A functionalist orientation views a society as an integrated whole with all of its practices and institutions working together harmoniously to fulfill individual needs or to sustain the society in a state of equilibrium. Despite the very different approaches of social evolutionism and functionalism to studying human behavior, when it came to arguments about gender roles, little had actually changed.

Adherents to functionalism, for example, continued to invoke biological factors in their explanation of women's roles around the world. For example, E. E. Evans-Pritchard, a leading British functionalist, contended that regardless of the variety of social institutions found in different societies, men were always in the ascendancy, occupying roles of authority based on "deep biological and psychological factors" (1965:55). Women's lives in all societies, he contended, naturally centered on home and family due to their role in procreation, while men's focused on activities of public importance. Evans-Pritchard claimed that this natural division of labor allowed a society to function harmoniously and to maintain the balance necessary for its continued successful functioning, a claim that conveniently discounted the demands for equality being made by the British women's movement at the time of Evans-Pritchard's writing. Like the social evolutionists they otherwise discounted, anthropologists who used a functionalist point of view assumed that both women's exclusion from the public realm and male dominance were natural and necessary. Yet, these theorists spent little time actually investigating the variation in, and importance of, women's roles in non-Western societies.

THE FEMINIST CRITIQUE OF FUNCTIONALISM

By the 1970s, feminist anthropologists began to point out functionalist shortcomings and to question anthropological assumptions about male superiority, seeing them as a reflection of widespread male bias in the discipline (Reiter 1975a; Sacks 1974; Slocum 1975). This bias had led social evolutionists and functionalists to assume that what women did was unimportant and thus to overlook women's activities in their writing. Feminist anthropologists contended that the ethnographic data from which such conclusions were drawn were based on questions that (mostly) male anthropologists asked men about their daughters and wives. This practice led Rayna (Rapp) Reiter to remark that, in anthropology, "what women do is perceived as household work and what they talk about is called gossip, while men's work is viewed as the economic base of society and their information is seen as important social communication" (1975b:12).

With the rise of feminist anthropology, many women anthropologists set out to rectify this lack of interest in women's lives . By focusing in their ethnographic work on what women do, on how gender roles and behaviors differ across societies, and on the significance of women's work in many societies, they called into question the androcentric biases that plagued early anthropological accounts.

In the United States, this functionalist view concerning gender issues persists even today. For example, a *New York Times* front-page article, "U.S. Colleges Begin to Ask, Where Have the Men Gone," recently reported growing anxiety over the steady increase of women on college campuses (Lewin 1998). Citing predictions that by the year 2007, 9.2 million women will be enrolled compared to 6.9 million men, the article raised concerns about the continued smooth functioning of a society in which men's economic opportunities will be limited in comparison to women's. In good functionalist style, the article equates men with society and suggests that something is wrong when society no longer meets the needs of its population in the same way that it did in the past.

MORE RECENT EVOLUTIONARY ARGUMENTS

Like social evolutionists, more contemporary anthropologists using evolutionary models to understand gender roles and behaviors seek explanations in *biological* differences between the sexes. Social evolutionists, as we have seen, were interested in explaining how some societies became more "fit" and thus more highly evolved than others. Since they saw their own societies as the most "fit," they concluded that the gender arrangements found in them were superior to those assumed to have existed in "less evolved" societies. Such explanations were then used to rationalize gender inequalities.

More recent evolutionary theorists are less interested in the evolution of societies than in the evolution of our particular species, *Homo sapiens*. They compare human behaviors and traits with those of such nonhuman primates as monkeys and apes. The similarities found between humans and these other species are understood as general primate characteristics. Those that differ are seen as uniquely human and are attributed to natural selection. In other words, evolutionary theorists argue that traits found only in humans must have arisen because they allowed our early human ancestors to adapt to environmental conditions and survive.

Evolutionary thinkers are generally in agreement that the most significant trait differentiating hominids—humans and their immediate ancestors—is bipedalism, or walking upright on two feet. Early theorists of this school tended to focus on the effect bipedalism had in freeing the hands for such quintessentially human behaviors as hunting. Perhaps the most well-known explanation of this idea is the one proposed by Sherwood Washburn and C. S. Lancaster in their 1968 article, "The Evolution of Hunting." While more recent theorists, like C. Owen Lovejoy (1981), still focus on bipedalism, they tend to emphasize its impact not on the ability to hunt but on the development of new reproductive behaviors. These theorists are especially concerned with the traits that they think might have allowed our species to procreate more successfully. Such explanations tend to draw on the principles E. O. Wilson formulated from his research on the social behavior of ants. Wilson's explanations are outlined in his influential book, *Sociobiology: The New Synthesis* (1975).

Wilson's underlying assumption is that the social behavior of animals, including humans, is largely genetically programmed. Sociobiologists are particularly concerned with what they see as the different
strategies men and women have developed over the course of evolution
to increase the likelihood that their genes will be passed on to later generations.

Even though newer models of human evolution draw on information that was unavailable to Washburn and Lancaster three decades
ago, these newer models still contain many of the same problematic
assumptions about gender and employ much of the same questionable
forms of reasoning. Washburn and Lancaster's model is thus a good
starting point for understanding even the most current evolutionary
explanations of gender roles and behaviors.

Man the Hunter

Washburn and Lancaster (1968) proposed what has come to be
known as the "man the hunter" model of human evolution. According to
them, "our intellect, interests, emotions, and basic social life . . . all are
products of the success of the hunting adaptation" (p. 293). This scenario
suggests that as a result of bipedalism, the hands of our hominid ancestors were freed, eventually leading to the ability of early humans to
hunt large game with tools or weapons. This ability exerted a force over
almost all aspects of human cultural behavior and social organization.
For example, Washburn and Lancaster assert that language arose
because it allowed successful communication among members of a
hunting party, while the manufacture of tools for hunting resulted in
increased brain size and the development of art. Washburn and Lancaster explain this relationship thus:

> There must have been strong selection for greater skill in manufac-
> ture and use [of tools], and it is no accident that the bones of small-
> brained men (*Australopithecus*) are never found with beautiful, sym-
> metrical tools. If the brains of contemporary apes and men are com-
> pared, the area associated with manual skills (both in cerebellum
> and cortex) are at least three times as large in man. Clearly the suc-
> cess of tools has exerted a great influence on the evolution of the
> brain, and has created the skills that make art possible. (1968:298)

The most significant aspect of the "man the hunter" model for
understanding gender roles is Washburn and Lancaster's assumption
that it was men who hunted large game, while women gathered vegetable foods and cared for dependent infants. This division of labor neces-
sitated the sharing of food resources between women and their offspring
and men. Food sharing provided the basis for the development of the
human family. According to Washburn and Lancaster, the family is "the

result of the reciprocity of hunting, the addition of a male to the mother-plus-young social group of monkeys and apes" (1968:301).

Washburn and Lancaster admit that there is no direct evidence that the human family arose deep in our evolutionary past. They speculate, however, that one unique aspect of human physiology suggests that it did. This factor is what is referred to as the "loss of estrus" in human females. Nonhuman primate females have a moment of heightened fertility when they ovulate once or twice a year. During these moments, sexual intercourse is more likely to result in conception. External signs, such as enlarged genitalia, that cue male partners to a female's readiness to mate often signal this period, known as estrus. In some animals, this time period is called "heat." Human females do not have these discrete moments and have lost the signs that signal ovulation. This change, Washburn and Lancaster contend, allowed human males to initiate intercourse with females at any time and led to the development of mechanisms to control women so that men could be assured of year-round sexual activity. Loss of an estrus period, according to this way of thinking, gives rise to pair-bonding, the development of long-term male-female bonds, which also contributed to the establishment of the family. Females acquiesced to male sexual desire to ensure that they and their children would be provisioned with the meat that males brought back from the hunt.

Washburn and Lancaster (1968) also claimed that hunting exerted a profound effect on human psychology (p. 299). Since they saw hunting as essential to human survival, they reasoned that it must have been easily learned and pleasurable. Language facilitated the transmission of ideas about hunting and thus made learning easier, while immediate enjoyment was the reward for killing. Washburn and Lancaster tell us that the satisfaction early men supposedly derived from the hunt is still evident today in the efforts made to maintain killing as a sport and in the pleasure men derive from participating in warfare (p. 299).

Woman the Gatherer

The problematic assumptions underlying "man the hunter" are many. Sally Slocum provided one of the earliest and most complete responses to it in a 1975 article entitled "Woman the Gatherer: Male Bias in Anthropology." Slocum contested the androcentric biases in Washburn and Lancaster's model, especially its assumption that behavior exclusive to men resulted in the evolution of all that we have come to think of as uniquely human. Slocum quotes Jane Kephart, another critic of this model, who has made clear the ramifications of this androcentric bias. The implications of the "man the hunter" model, according to Kephart, are that

since only males hunt, and the psychology of the species was set by
hunting, we are forced to conclude that females are scarcely human,
that is, do not have built-in the basic psychology of the species: to kill
and hunt and ultimately to kill others of the same species. The argument implies built-in aggression in human males, as well as the assumed passivity of human females and their exclusion from the
mainstream of human development. (in Slocum 1975:38)

Slocum demonstrates that the same aspects of human culture and
social organization that Washburn and Lancaster attribute to the
"hunting way of life" can be explained with reference to the "gathering
way of life." Among nonhuman primates, food is not shared between
males and females, and mothers feed infants not by sharing food with
them but by nursing them. During the course of human evolution, the
period of an infant's dependency on its mother increased, requiring
mothers to share food with their children in order to ensure their survival. Thus, food sharing would have developed, according to Slocum,
not because men shared meat with women, but because mothers shared
gathered food with their children, both male and female. This behavior
probably predated hunting, since gathering is the basis of the diet of all
primates. Moreover, as Slocum points out, there is no solid empirical evidence to suggest that sharing would have arisen only with the development of a sexual division of labor, one in which women gathered exclusively and men hunted, as Washburn and Lancaster assumed.

Over the course of human evolution, longer pregnancies, more difficult births, and a lengthened period of infant dependency would have
required "more skills in social organization and communication—creating selective pressure for increased brain size" (Slocum 1975:46). Thus
Slocum argues we need not look to hunting as an explanation for these
aspects of human life. Furthermore, the first tools used by humans may
not have been for the purpose of hunting but for gathering food and caring
for children—digging sticks, food storage containers, or slings and nets to
carry babies. Such tools would have enabled more efficient food gathering
and accumulation. Early hominid procurement strategies also demanded
specialized knowledge, including knowledge of the location and identification of plant varieties and of seasonal and geographic changes, knowledge more easily transmitted through language (Slocum 1975:47).

Slocum not only critiques the "man the hunter" hypothesis for its
androcentrism, but for its unwarranted leaps of logic. She points out, for
example, that "the emphasis on hunting as a prime moving factor in
hominid evolution distorts the data," and she argues that "it is simply
too big a jump to go from the primate individual-gathering pattern to a
hominid cooperative hunting-sharing pattern without [hypothesizing]
some intervening changes" (Slocum 1975:48).

Slocum has also pointed to the problematic assumptions that the
"man the hunter" model contains about female sexuality. She suggests

that in most primate groups it is the female who initiates sexual inter-course, not the male. It is Western male bias, she claims, that infers that early male hominids both chose a female and maintained control over her and her offspring to ensure a man's sexual access to her. According to Slocum, the presumption that the long-term commitment of one male to one female is an old, established pattern is contradicted by evidence that shows that long-term monogamy is a relatively rare pattern even among modern humans (Slocum 1975:43). The work of feminist archae-ologists such as Margaret Conkey (1997) and Joan Gero (1985) have fur-thered Slocum's pioneering work, calling into question traditional assumptions about prehistoric gender roles and pointing to the com-plexities involved in reconstructing gender relations in past societies.

Lovejoy's Model of Human Evolution

Even though Washburn and Lancaster's model was seriously crit-icized as long ago as 1975, newer evolutionary models contain many of its problematic claims and assumptions. While newer models no longer emphasize hunting as the prime mover in human evolution, they con-tinue to focus on the role that supposedly human characteristics, such as pair-bonding, the nuclear family, and loss of estrus, have played in the development of our species. A well-known example of this type of model is the one developed by Lovejoy (1981). Lovejoy's model has been widely disseminated by Donald Johanson and Maitland Edey, who draw on it in their popular book, *Lucy: The Beginnings of Humankind* (1981a).

According to Lovejoy, "for any quadruped to get up on its hind legs in order to run is an insane thing to do," since bipedalism is an ineffi-cient form of locomotion (quoted in Johanson and Edey 1981b:309). Bipedalism arose, nonetheless. It evolved, according to Lovejoy, to solve what he calls the demographic dilemma of apes. This dilemma resulted from the reproductive strategy used by apes, one referred to as K-selec-tion. As Johanson and Edey explain:

> There are two fundamentally different ways in which an animal can function sexually: It can produce a great many eggs with an invest-ment of very little energy in any one egg, or it can produce very few eggs with a large investment in each. These are known as the "r" strategy and the "K" strategy respectively . . . "K" is obviously far more efficient than "r," but it too has its limits. Accidents, predation, seasonal food failure, illness-all take their toll on animals. Losing an infant to one of these hazards after an investment of five or six years is hideously costly compared with the loss of an egg by [an r strategy animal]. (1981b:46)

Lovejoy hypothesizes that apes, including those which were the ancestors of humans, were dangerously "K" selected; that is, they were perilously close to extinction because they invested a large amount of energy in the rearing of a very few children. Such a focused investment could be disastrous if only a few infants died each year. According to Lovejoy, hominids were able to avoid this fate, and to become the most successful primate, by speeding up their birthrate. This resulted in more overlap among children and required that mothers care for more than one baby at a time. To do so, they needed to restrict their movements and direct the energy saved by sedentism to caring for children. Rearing more children required females to become dependent on males to provide food for them and their offspring. The reward for such sharing, Lovejoy argues, was sex.

When males and females come together in primate species to copulate, at least according to Lovejoy, competition and fighting among males often occur. Thus, he reasons, mechanisms must have evolved to reduce conflict. This reduction in male competition was accomplished through the loss of estrus, which made females sexually available to males year round, facilitating long-term pair-bonding. With the loss of obvious external signals of ovulation, accompanied by the loss of estrus, Lovejoy argues, a female began to depend on permanent features of her body, such as her hair, skin, breasts, and shape, to attract a male. As Johanson and Edey put it, the estrus flag no longer counts, since the female has permanent ones to keep her man—her hominid—interested in her all the time (1981b:48). Johanson and Edey summarize Lovejoy's model thus:

> There are always ways of defusing male [aggression due to competition for mates]. . . . One is to lower the competition for sex. If each male has his own female, *his own private gene receptacle*, he doesn't have to fight with other males for representation in succeeding generations. More parental care and food sharing become possible. As a result, the females can afford to become less mobile. If the primate becomes less mobile . . . it can become more bipedal. . . . Because it doesn't have to run as much, it can afford to be less efficient in order to do other things that begin to have survival value—like carrying the extra food needed to nurture extra children. If a male is now walking upright, he's better equipped to carry food and more likely to bring it to the female (1981b:47–48, emphasis added)

Critique of Lovejoy's Model

In this scenario, women are seen as necessarily dependent on males for their survival. They are also characterized as sex objects, seen as attractive to males for the very traits Western men like Lovejoy, Johanson, and Edey find desirable in women. Such conclusions are highly ethnocentric. Studies of the sexual behavior of nonhuman primates, moreover, reveal that sexual activity outside a female's period of maximum fertility is not an exclusive characteristic of human sexuality (see Burton 1972; Hrdy 1979; Manson 1986; and Rowell 1972).

Contemporary gender roles, behaviors, and expectations are thus projected back into the evolutionary past and seen as being at the very foundation of the survival and evolution of humans. It should be clear that Lovejoy's emphasis on a female dependency/male-provisioning model is strikingly similar to that of Washburn and Lancaster. Both models are questionable given ethnographic evidence of female mobility in hunting and gathering societies. Among foragers, women with infants often range over large areas in search of vegetable foods, which make up the largest proportion of the diet for most hunting and gathering groups. Moreover, women do hunt and routinely capture small animals as they gather, contributing meat to the diet. Evidence from the archaeological record also contradicts the assumption that there is an inherent sexual division of labor. As Lila Leibowitz (1983) has remarked, "the artifacts and early detritus associated with early human groups . . . reflect the use of foraging techniques that are simple, involve both sexes and call for similar activities on the part of both" (p. 136).

Many anthropologists have also questioned whether early hominids were in a K-trap, experiencing a demographic dilemma requiring an increase in birth rate and infant survivorship. They suggest that there is no solid evidence to support this contention (see, for example, Harley 1982; Isaac 1982; Wood 1982).

Why, then, in the face of such problematic assumptions and such paltry data, has Lovejoy's model and others like it received such warm acceptance by a popular audience? Many scholars have suggested that this popularity is due to the way such speculations reinforce cultural assumptions about men's and women's roles. Projecting contemporary Western behaviors into the evolutionary past provides a rationale for their continued existence.

Articles proposing a female dependency/male-provisioning model are more likely to be published in popular magazines like *Newsweek*, *Psychology Today*, and *Science Digest*, while refutations of these arguments remain buried in obscure and less-frequently read scientific journals. Evolutionary models posited by sociobiologists are especially favored by the popular press. Sociobiologists are even more directly concerned with the evolution of human sexual behaviors than researchers like Lovejoy and are even guiltier of assuming that Western gender relations and behaviors are universal and, therefore, evolutionarily advantageous.

Sociobiology and Selfish Genes

Rather than understanding human reproductive strategies as ones that benefited the species of *Homo sapiens* as a whole, sociobiologists see male-female sexual relations as a contest between men and women. This "battle of the sexes," as they call it, has arisen over the course of evolution because men and women must develop competing reproductive strategies to ensure that their genes will be passed on. These strategies are, in turn, the result of the differences in the biology of males and females. As sociobiologist Richard Dawkins explains, male and female gender behavior is motivated by selfish genes. That is, males and females can be thought of as trying to exploit the other, trying to force the other one to invest more in their offspring in order to optimize the chances that their own genes will be passed down to future generations (Dawkins 1976:150).

According to sociobiology, there is a disparity in the investment men and women must make in the rearing of children to ensure the child's survival and, thus, the survival of their own genes. Differing degrees of this parental investment arise from the fact that a female's egg, or ovum, is much larger than a male's sperm, requiring more energy investment for its production, and because women get pregnant and men do not. Dawkins has made the importance of the different size of ova and sperm clear, stating that it is possible to interpret all the other differences between the sexes as stemming from this one basic difference (1976:152).

Men and women therefore develop different reproductive strategies. Sociobiological accounts propose that males can optimize their genetic fitness, the chances of passing on their genes, by impregnating as many females as possible. Males are thus genetically programmed, according to sociobiologists, for a hyper-sexuality, one that encourages them to philander and to have frequent sex with multiple partners.

Women, so this scenario suggests, are chaste by comparison. Once pregnant, more frequent sexual relations will not increase a woman's chances of successfully passing on her genes, since she can only be pregnant once at a time. Once her child is born, according to sociobiologists, a female increases the chances of her investment paying off by investing even more time and energy in the rearing of her child. To relieve some of this burden, sociobiologists argue, a woman attempts to encourage a man to help her care for her dependent child. Even with this help, it is not in the woman's self-interest to abandon her child to a male caretaker in order to be impregnated again by a different male. For a female must fear that if she leaves her baby in a man's care, his relatively small investment in the child might cause him to abandon it completely. She risks losing her investment entirely. Women benefit from male help but must develop a means to keep the male around so that he does not merely leave her in order to spread more of his own genes.

To keep the male around, women engage in a domestic-bliss strategy, one that depends on her playing hard to get in the mating game. By being coy and holding out on sex, the female is likely to attract a male willing to wait. It is in the female's interest to find such a man, since he might also be more willing to stick around after the birth of a child than a man who wants sex without commitment. Long courtship periods also aid the male who is in less danger of being duped into believing that a child is his when a woman has really been impregnated by another male. Having invested so heavily in courtship, the male optimizes the return on his investment by remaining committed to his coy female partner.

Coy females, and more-or-less faithful males, are thus the ones most likely to rear children successfully and pass on their genes. What may have begun as an idiosyncratic reproductive pattern becomes stabilized in the population once enough females play the game. As Dawkins argues,

> when coy females increase in numbers so much that they predomi-
> nate, the philanderer males, who had such an easy time with fast fe-
> males, start to feel the pinch. Female after female insists on a long
> and arduous courtship. The philanderers flit from female to female,
> and always the story is the same. The net pay-off for the philanderer
> male when all the females are coy is zero. (1976:164)

Nevertheless, since no system is perfect, loose, fast females will always exist, tempting men to increase their genetic fitness by copulating with them, even if the men are monogamously bonded to other women. Faithful wives and less faithful husbands are thus the product of natural selection. The genes giving rise to these behaviors have been selected for during the course of human evolutionary history.

Critique of Sociobiology

As we have suggested, the characteristics associated with males and females in the selfish gene model are strikingly similar to those that exist in contemporary Western societies. Until the sexual revolution of the 1960s in the United States, for example, women were expected to be virgins at the time of marriage, a trait that was highly valued. Male indiscretions, by contrast, were not cause for alarm or disparagement. Even today in the age of AIDS, when any promiscuous sexual behavior is dangerous, highly sexually active women in North American society are often viewed more contemptuously than highly sexually active males. A man enjoys a double standard and need not fear being labeled a slut, a whore, or loose.

Do men everywhere actually have a more active sex drive than women? According to Fatima Mernissi (1987), in Morocco women are viewed as more highly sexed than men. There, men fear the intensity of female sexuality, seeing it as capable of distracting them from their dedication to God. The existence of societies in which men have sex more often than women does not provide proof of the naturalness of an intense male sex drive and a passive female one, as sociobiologists claim. Because women experience the consequences of pregnancy more directly, they may have stronger *societal* sanctions against frequent sex, not internal genetic mechanisms regulating it (see Mascia-Lees, Tierson, and Relethford 1989).

The sociobiological model can also be questioned for its assumption that there is differential investment in a child at the moment of its conception since female ova are bigger than male sperm. This assumption may be warranted for species in which the size of the female gamete is large in relation to total body size, but not necessarily in humans where the energy needed to produce male and female gametes is minimal. Moreover, human females are born with all of their ova, while men must continuously produce sperm. Sociobiologists have not yet produced studies measuring the differential energy required in the maturation of eggs versus the production of sperm, even though, as we have seen, they base their entire explanation of the evolution of gender roles and behaviors on this assumption (see Fedigan 1982 for a more detailed discussion of the egg-sperm fallacy).

The reasoning in sociobiological models is much like that found in nineteenth-century social evolutionary accounts. As social evolutionists used their own societies as the starting point of their analysis, assuming their inherent superiority, so sociobiologists today use themselves and the behaviors found in their own societies as a universal reference point. They make unwarranted generalizations about the universality of their own society's sexual norms, such as the coyness of females, and then suggest that because these traits are universal, they must have come about during the long evolutionary history of humans.

Unlike most cultural anthropologists, sociobiologists frequently take a behavior out of its cultural context and assume that if a certain behavior in another culture looks the same as one in their own, it must mean the same thing. Anthropologists have repeatedly shown the pitfalls of this thinking. Even something as simple as a wink, for example, can have many different meanings associated with it and may not carry the meaning of flirtation that many Westerners attribute to it (see Geertz 1973).

Feminist Evolutionary Models

Feminist anthropologists interested in the evolution of human behavior have not only provided critiques of sociobiology but have also offered alternative evolutionary models that do not rely on the problematic assumptions so deeply embedded in sociobiological accounts (see, for example, Fedigan 1982; Hrdy 1981; Morbeck, Galloway, and Zihlman 1997; Tanner 1981). Nancy Tanner and Adrienne Zihlman (1976) have shown the key role female primates and hominids played in the development of human behavior. Fran Mascia-Lees and her colleagues (1986) have provided a model of the evolution of permanently enlarged breasts in humans that does not depend on viewing women as sex objects whose breasts evolved to attract males. A number of researchers have focused on the importance of friendship, rather than sexual attraction, in binding males and females together both in primate groups (see, for example, Smuts 1985) and in early hominid societies (see, for example, Cohen and Mascia-Lees 1989).

Evolutionary Psychology

Currently in vogue is a field called evolutionary psychology whose stated aim is to generate good theories of personality development (Wright 1994:82). While proponents of this discipline criticize earlier sociobiologists for their reductive reasoning—that is, for attributing all human behaviors to simplistic genetic mechanisms—their own models differ in only the slightest of ways. Their explanations for the evolution of gender behaviors are almost identical to those proposed by earlier writers, such as Washburn and Lancaster, Lovejoy, Wilson, and Dawkins.

For example, Robert Wright's model as proposed in *The Moral Animal: Evolutionary Psychology in Everyday Life* (1994) includes all the familiar references. He proposes a genetic basis for human social behavior; he draws on the female dependency/male provider concept; he points to women's use of their sexuality to attract and exploit men; he hypothesizes genetic payoffs for optimal mating strategies; and he invokes the battle of the sexes scenario. Wright's evolutionary account differs from earlier sociobiological ones, however, in the emphasis it places on the imprint such evolutionary behaviors exert on the minds, or psychology, of humans.

Evolutionary psychologists also tend to claim that there is more complexity in the genetic mechanisms underlying reproductive strategies than earlier sociobiologists recognized. For example, complex traits like human sexuality, Wright tells us, "result from the interaction of numerous genes, each of which, typically, was selected for its incremental addition to fitness" (1994:57). Thus, rather than a simple "selfish gene" dictating human behavior, Wright envisions multiple genes coming together, as if they were knights at the round table, to "counsel" individuals in the behavioral strategies most beneficial to them. Yet, Wright and other evolutionary psychologists are even further from being able to identify a complex set of genes than sociobiologists are from finding that single selfish gene. Wright's view of male and female sexual behavior is even more stereotypic and replete with Western bias than earlier accounts. Moreover, his suggestions that "males will have sex with just about anything that moves given an easy chance" (1994:64) and that males are maniacally jealous (p. 70) portray men in questionable and unflattering terms. His reference to human babies as "mounds of helpless flesh" (p. 58) depersonalizes human beings, portraying them in ways that are unlikely to shed much light on such complex creatures.

THE GENE AS CULTURAL ICON

Feminist anthropologists have been particularly wary of evolutionary explanations of gender behaviors and differences because of the Western-centered, untested assumptions that they contain. Moreover, as we suggested in chapter 1, models that attribute gender behaviors to biological and natural causes but are based on no solid empirical evidence are more likely to reflect the cultural assumptions of the writer than to uncover the actual processes that give rise to gender arrangements. Donna Haraway (1990, 1991) has shown that gender and race hierarchies are frequently underwritten by cultural myths masquerading as factual, objective, scientific theories.

Nonetheless, as we have also pointed out, biological explanations continue to fascinate many researchers as well as the general public. Dorothy Nelkin and M. Susan Lindee (1995) suggest that this is due to the "gene" becoming the new cultural icon for North American society. References to DNA and genes now dominate popular culture. "Gene talk," Nelkin and Lindee demonstrate, "has entered the vernacular as a subject for drama, a source of humor, and an explanation of human behavior" (1995:1–2). As they point out in supermarket tabloids and soap operas, in television sitcoms and talk shows, genes appear to explain everything, including obesity, criminality, shyness, directional ability, intelligence, political leanings, preferred styles of dress, and, as you may recall from chapter 1, the propensity of liberals to wear beards. Nelkin and Lindee suggest that DNA and the gene function in many respects as the secular equivalent of the Christian soul; they are seen as independent and immortal, as fundamental to identity, to the moral order, and even to human fate (p. 2). They point out that geneticists refer to the genome, the totality of human genetic material, as the Bible, the Holy Grail, and the Book of Man (p. 8).

As Nelkin and Lindee also indicate, efforts to measure the relative influence of nature versus nurture on human behavior are highly controversial and problematic. Quoting the evolutionary biologist, Stephen J. Gould, they write that

> genes may influence many aspects of human behavior, but we cannot say that such behavior is caused by genes in any direct way. We cannot even claim that a given behavior is, say, 40% genetic and 60% environmental. . . . Genes and environment interact in a non-additive way. (Gould quoted in Nelkin and Lindee 1995:10)

African Americans have been particularly sensitive to claims about the importance of genes to human behavior, given the racist uses to which claims of a biological basis to racial differences have been put historically. Many women have been similarly wary of claims that gender behaviors are genetically determined due to historical precedents, such as those set by social evolutionists. However, genetic models, even when largely unsubstantiated, capture many people's attention, providing simple and seemingly straightforward explanations for the behaviors that occur in an increasingly complex world.

Genetic models also are often directed toward explaining behaviors whose implications for social policy are large, such as who or which group might make best use of limited economic resources. At the same time, attributing unsavory behavior, such as rape or male infidelity, to genes, as some authors have (see *Science Digest* 1982:64), precludes individual accountability. Individuals need not be personally responsible for their actions if it is their uncontrollable genes that produce such behavior.

CONCLUSIONS

Evolutionary models, with their problematic assumptions and faulty reasoning, have dominated biological explanations of gender within anthropology. However, data gathered by researchers in other fields may point to the possible biological basis of some behaviors. In *The Two Sexes* (1998), for example, the psychologist Eleanor Maccoby reviews work done in the area of developmental social psychology that suggests that the segregation of boys and girls into same-sex play groups is universal, suggesting that a biological mechanism is at work. In the absence of direct data to confirm this interpretation, however, the conclusion that there is a biological basis for this social behavior remains tentative. Given the provisional nature of such data, and the use to which biological arguments for gender differences have been put historically, many feminist anthropologists have been wary of jumping to conclusions about the biological basis of social behavior. Perhaps as more concrete and direct evidence accumulates, it will be possible to substantiate claims that certain behaviors are under some type of biological control. Until that time, however, most anthropologists continue to be suspicious of unsubstantiated arguments about the biological basis of human behavior.

In the history of the discipline, most anthropologists have looked to social factors, not solely biological causes, to explain gender differences in behavior and the causes of sexual stratification. It is to these kinds of explanations that we turn in the rest of this book.

Chapter Four

The Psychological
Orientation

A major focus of the psychologically oriented anthropological literature concerned with gender has been on explanations of the differences that characterize male and female personality types. Anthropologists have been particularly concerned with identifying the cultural factors that shape the development of these traits and that underlie sex role behaviors.

The interest in defining and specifying the exact nature of the personality differences between the sexes has its roots in Freudian psychology. Freud, like other nineteenth-century thinkers, was steeped in the assumption of the natural inferiority of women. While Freud's work has been seriously criticized by some feminists because of this assumption, many others have taken his focus on the "family drama," which he saw as underlying personality formation, as a starting point for their own explanations of gender identity. However, feminist models of this type do not depend on Freud's androcentric assumption of male superiority. Other anthropologists have eschewed Freud's psychoanalytic approach entirely, focusing less on the infant-caretaker bond than on how the process of social learning, or socialization, affects the formation of gender identities.

This chapter explores Freud's ideas and his influence on feminist anthropology. This influence is especially evident in Nancy Chodorow's article, "Family Structure and Feminine Personality," which appeared in the founding text of feminist anthropology, *Woman, Culture, & Society* (1974). While Freud sought explanations for sex differences in personality in the biological differences between the sexes, Chodorow, like most other psychologically oriented anthropologists, has called this assumption into question. She suggests that cultural forces, not biological ones, are at work in the psychological formation of individuals. In this assumption, Chodorow is closer to the social learning theorists whose ideas we use to assess a number of Freud's assumptions and whose work we review at the end of this chapter.

FREUD'S PSYCHOANALYTIC APPROACH

Freud proposed two psychological developmental processes, the Oedipal complex and the Electra complex. According to him, in order for boys to develop proper masculine behaviors, they must learn to renounce their attachment to their mothers and to identify with their fathers. Freud termed this process the Oedipal conflict, naming it after the mythical Greek character, Oedipus, whose life was tragic because he killed his father and had sex with his mother. Girls, Freud argued, must undergo a different process, one that allows them to forgive their mothers for their inadequacy—the lack of a penis—and to re-establish an attachment with them. Freud called this process the Electra complex, naming it after the figure in Greek mythology who incites her brother Orestes to murder their mother.

According to Freud, every boy must resolve the Oedipal conflict in order to develop the appropriate masculine personality. A young boy who has an attachment to his mother as his first love object grows to desire sexual intercourse with her. Having the knowledge that women lack a penis, however, the boy dreads the same fate. He fears that his all-powerful father will castrate him if he acts on his sexual desires. This castration anxiety leads the boy to repress his sexual feelings for his mother, to reject her, and to disdain all women because they lack a penis. The boy also begins to identify with his father, leading him to model his father's behaviors and to develop a bond with him.

A girl undergoes a different version of this process of psychological development. She comes to recognize that she lacks a penis. Since her mother also does not have a penis, the young girl blames her mother for this shortcoming. The girl not only regards boys and men with envy because they have this organ but also rejects and disdains her mother and all other women for their lack of one (Freud [1933] 1965:589). Girls come to abhor their own mothers and see them as rivals for their father's attention.

Spurred on by penis envy, the girl remains in the Electra complex until she learns to identify with her mother as a symbolic means of possessing her father and, through this identification, obtaining the penis she desires. But since the girl does not identify directly with the father as a boy comes to do, she never develops the traits Freud associated with men: a clear sense of justice and the ability to work actively in the larger world.

Women are confined by this natural developmental process, which is based on their anatomical "lack," to the domestic sphere in which their penis envy is later mollified by "gaining" a penis through marrying a man and having male children. Women, according to Freud, are naturally dependent and passive. They are also masochistic and vain, hating themselves for what they lack and trying to compensate for it by making themselves beautiful and desirable in other ways. Thus, according to the Freudian model, women are naturally inferior to men and will remain that way. For Freud, "anatomy is destiny."

CHODOROW'S PSYCHOANALYTIC MODEL

Nancy Chodorow (1974) has both challenged and expanded Freud's theory. She was interested in explaining, as Freud was, what she presumed were "nearly universal differences that characterize masculine and feminine personality and roles" (p. 43). She did not, however, turn to biology to explain this occurrence, nor did she agree with Freud that such universal personality traits necessarily doomed women to a position of inferiority to men. Instead, she argued that the consequences of male and female personality traits depended upon a society's particular interpretation of them. Indeed, Chodorow's work has been an important impetus for research in feminist anthropology on the *cultural* and *social* factors influencing psychological development and gender identity.

According to Chodorow (1974), personality development is a result of relational experiences developed in infancy, which become generalized as one grows older. Chodorow claimed that the critical factor giving rise to the different experiences males and females have as infants is that women are responsible for child care. While both male and female infants have an early identification with their mothers, a mother will tend to identify more closely with her daughters. By contrast, a mother will push her son away, emphasizing a boy's masculinity in opposition to her own femininity. A boy therefore becomes more differentiated from his mother than does a girl. Moreover, Chodorow claimed, a boy has to learn to identify with a more distant father. A boy thus identifies with diffuse and generalized male traits rather than with an actual individual. All these factors contribute to the establishment of strong and rigid boundaries between self and other in boys, making them more independent and self-reliant than girls.

In contrast, a girl's gender identification is of a more personal nature. It is based on close identification with her mother, the person with whom she has had a genuine and continual relationship since infancy. This intimacy results in a girl never completely rejecting her mother in favor of men. The feminine personality, then, is founded on relation and connections, producing a secure sense of gender identity and more flexible boundaries between self and other than males have.

These traits can cause problems for women in societies that do not value women, according to Chodorow. For example, in societies in which women have low status, the process of gender formation will require girls to identify with a devalued figure. In this case, a girl's rejection of her mother also involves the "rejection and devaluation of herself, because of her pre-Oedipal identification and boundary confusion with her mother" (Chodorow 1974:65). By contrast, in societies in which women have important kinship roles or influential authority, women will not be devalued. Therefore, a girl's close identification with her mother will not be problematic. While Chodorow agrees with Freud that male and female personality types are universal and determined by gender, she disagrees with Freud's idea that gender development will always result in women being considered inferior to men.

CRITIQUE OF FREUDIAN ASSUMPTIONS

Unfortunately, neither Chodorow nor Freud provides clear evidence that male and female personality types are universal across all cultures. Clinical studies suggest that there is no evidence to support such a generalization (Maccoby and Jacklin 1974), and some researchers have suggested that there may be more personality differences among individuals than between males and females (see, for example, Freize, et al. 1978:2).

One study has found that traits traditionally associated in Western culture with women, such as nurturance and a sense of responsibility for others, and with men, such as independence and dominance, vary not by sex but by women's labor responsibilities. In a study of six cultures, Whiting and Whiting (1975) found that where women perform many necessary subsistence tasks that are arduous and time consuming, children, regardless of gender, will be organized to help and responsibility for others will be stressed. Nurturance training is also emphasized for children regardless of the sex of the caregiver if children are caregivers themselves. There is also widespread evidence that children do not necessarily identify with the parent of the same sex as Freud assumed.

Freud's ideas have also been criticized for their androcentric bias: he took males as the norm and saw anyone who deviated from this norm as pathological or inferior. He characterized men by what they possess and held them in high regard because of it. Women were defined by what they lack, not by what they have.

While many studies have provided refutation of some of Freud's assertions, it is important to remember that many are also indebted to him. Freud's ideas have been crucial for turning attention to the profound effect the early child-caretaker relationship can have on a child's psychological development. This insight has permeated studies of psychological development in a wide range of fields and has influenced the work of many feminists interested in the complicated effects of childhood bonding.

SOCIAL LEARNING THEORY

As we discussed in chapter 2, theorists who approach the development of gender identity and behavior using a social learning orientation focus on how cultural learning shapes male and female personality types. Early studies of this type tended to focus on the necessity in most societies of aligning male and female personality characteristics with the responsibilities that adult men and women have in productive activities. For example, Barry, Bacon, and Child (1957:328–29) proposed that the tendency in many societies to stress nurturance, obedience, and responsibility in girls is related to women's adult role in child rearing. In contrast, since men in many societies tend to participate in economic activities that take them farther from home, self-reliance and achievement striving will be stressed in boys. The six-culture study conducted by Whiting and Whiting mentioned above, however, found a woman's workload to be the most significant factor affecting personality type.

Recently, Eleanor Maccoby (1998) has called into question the assumption that the direct and conscious socialization efforts of parents are responsible for making boys masculine and girls feminine (p. 8). She argues that this approach is not wrong, but too limited. According to Maccoby:

> We now know that there are powerful gender-linked phenomena that do not fit into the traditional [socialization] framework. They can not be understood in terms of sex-typed personality traits or disposition inculcated in each individual child through the process of socialization. . . . Sex-linked behavior turns out to be a pervasive function of the social context in which it occurs. . . .We can point to a specific aspect of context which has broad relevance and which indeed is cross-culturally universal. It turns out that the relevant condition is the gender composition of the social pair or group within which the individual is functioning at any given time. The gendered aspect of an individual's behavior is brought into play by the gender of others. (1998:9)

Maccoby (1998) suggests that there is a strong tendency for children to seek out playmates of the same sex and that there are significant differences in the way children interact within all-male or all-female playgroups. Within all-male groups, boys are more likely to take risks, play rough, strive for dominance, confront others, and resist revealing their weaknesses to one another. In all-female groups, girls disclose more about themselves to others in the group, participate in more reciprocal and sustained discussions, avoid conflict, and pay more attention to maintaining positive social relations (p. 289). These contexts give rise to distinct interactive styles. Such "interactive repertoires," which are learned in same-sex groups, Maccoby asserts, will be used for same-sex interaction throughout an individual's lifetime. Cross-sex interaction will be affected by a wide range of factors, including the context in which male-female interactions occur and the nature of a society's cultural expectations surrounding male and female roles and behavior (p. 304).

THIRD GENDER CATEGORIES

Psychological anthropologists have also been interested in the variation in sexual identity found cross-culturally. Of particular interest to these anthropologists are societies in which men and women are not forced to conform to two strictly defined gender identities but are allowed to act as a "third gender" category. Among the Hijras of north India, for example, males who dress in women's clothing and act more like women than men are considered neither male nor female and perform special ritual functions (Nanda 1990). In Thailand, too, a man can take on the personality, dress, and behavior more often associated with women and can take either a man or a woman as his sexual partner (Morris 1994). Third gender categories also existed in many native societies of the United States and Canada before the nineteenth and twentieth centuries (Callender and Kochems 1983; Jacobs, Thomas, and Lang 1997). Whether such individuals are honored or abhorred by other members of their society depends upon the particular cultural context in which they exist.

The work on third gender categories has been important for undermining the idea that there is a natural connection between biological sex, defined in terms of bodily characteristics such as chromosomes or genitalia, and gender identity. This focus on how the body is complexly related to sexual and gender identity has been influential in shifting attention toward psychoanalytical explanations of selfhood (Harvey 1998:79).

CONCLUSIONS

The work of psychologically oriented anthropologists has revealed a high degree of plasticity in gender identities and suggests that cultural context and both direct and indirect socialization have a significant effect on the development of personality types. Much recent work in anthropology has tended to focus less on gender differences in personality than on the way in which an individual develops a sense of him- or herself. We turn our attention to such studies of identity formation in chapter 7.

Chapter Five

The Materialist Orientation

The social evolutionists discussed at the beginning of chapter 3 were not the only nineteenth-century thinkers to employ an evolutionary framework to explain differences in men's and women's roles and status. Among others were the social philosophers Karl Marx and Friedrich Engels. Like the social evolutionists, Marx and Engels hoped to uncover universal laws governing historical change and proposed a sequence of societal stages. Unlike the social evolutionists who sought to affirm Western civilization's naturalness and superiority, Marx and Engels sought to uncover the origins of its systems of oppression. They focused on the inequalities brought by the development of capitalism in Western societies.

While Marx is best known for his analyses of class oppression, Engels is perhaps best recognized for his treatment of gender oppression in his classic study, *The Origin of the Family, Private Property and the State* (1884), a book whose influence can still be felt today. While the evolutionary model Engels used in this text, and some of the assumptions underlying it, have been rejected, his basic approach has not. His focus on how the material conditions of life and economic factors affect gender stratification is still a starting point for materialist researchers today.

This chapter traces materialist explanations of systems of gender stratification from Marx's and Engels' views, especially the early model developed by Friedrich Engels, to those of contemporary theorists who have drawn on this work in their analyses. Our effort is to isolate those factors in Engels' account that have been invoked most often by contemporary writers and to document the way in which his original formulation has been refined, qualified, and expanded by them.

FOUNDATIONS OF MATERIALIST EXPLANATIONS OF GENDER

Karl Marx and Friedrich Engels ([1848] 1967) proposed that societies evolved from one stage of social organization to another. Different forms of property ownership characterized each stage, as did different modes or forms of labor and different means of production (the physical resources used in economic activities, such as land and tools). Marx and Engels hypothesized that in early societies production was based on the foraging of foodstuffs from the environment, and productive resources were shared in common by the entire group. Under such conditions of tribal ownership, as Marx and Engels called them, relationships among members were essentially egalitarian. With increases in population, however, societies grew into ones that eventually instituted private property ownership. Once ownership of such resources as land was no longer shared equally by all, distinctions within these societies arose.

This movement away from communal forms of property ownership toward private property ownership had reached its height, according to Marx and Engels, in the capitalist societies of their time (see especially Marx 1992). These societies were founded on an industrial base and were characterized by deep divisions that excluded a large portion of the population from access to resources and privileges. Under capitalism, two distinct classes had emerged: the bourgeoisie, who owned the means of production, and the proletariat, who worked for the owners and sold their labor to the bourgeoisie in exchange for wages.

Marx and Engels ([1848] 1967) viewed the exchange of labor for money in capitalist societies as inherently exploitative. Owners never paid workers what their labor was worth, because if they did, they would not make a profit. The bourgeoisie used this surplus value produced by members of the proletariat to further their own position. Marx and Engels saw capitalist-productive relationships as exploitative and alienating in yet another way. According to them, productive work was pleasurable when workers were able to reap the fruits of their own labor. Indeed, they saw productive labor as the very thing that differentiated humans from other animals. They contended it was responsible for the development of human consciousness. Toiling for wages, by contrast, divided workers from the products of their own labor, alienating them not only from their work but from themselves as well.

Marx and Engels ([1848] 1967) also argued that a society's economic base, or infrastructure, determined its superstructure—the legal, political, social, and cultural institutions that developed to ensure the continuation of the economic *status quo*. They saw these institutions as corresponding, in turn, to particular forms of social consciousness, determining the very way people thought about the world and themselves. The singular importance granted to the notion of individuality in Western European societies since the seventeenth-century, for example, can be tied, in a Marxist analysis, to the demands of a developing capitalism. In order to sell their labor, people needed to think of themselves as distinct from a larger social group, able and entitled as individuals to make decisions based on their own interests alone. Similarly, the increasing value in many Western societies over the last century placed on having young couples start their own households after marriage can be understood from a Marxist perspective in terms of the advantages it creates for a capitalist economy. If every individual household must have its own refrigerator and washing machine, for example, more products can be sold than if members of an extended family live together sharing expenses.

The division between owners and workers in Western capitalist societies would eventually lead to a class struggle so severe, according to Marx and Engels, that revolution would occur, and the establishment of a system of shared ownership, or communism, would once again be instituted. They envisioned this communistic society as one free of all exploitation and oppression, one in which people were no longer alienated from their labor and themselves, and one in which an entirely new human consciousness would arise. Marx and Engels outlined how, with this new consciousness, women would no longer be viewed as "mere instruments of production."

ENGELS' EVOLUTIONARY ACCOUNT

Engels began his analysis of gender oppression with the premise that the roles and position of men and women varied in time and space depending upon the economic relationships that characterized a particular society. He claimed that the movement away from the communal ownership of property found in early societies toward the private property ownership associated with class societies corresponded to the movement from higher to lower status for women.

Communal Society and Women's Position

In early communal societies in which everything produced was held in common, women enjoyed a high position. They performed important subsistence functions compatible with childbearing and child rearing, while men performed other necessary tasks. In a society in which paternity was unknown, descent was matrilineal, traced through women who were highly esteemed for their role as mothers. As Engels put it:

> The communistic household implies the supremacy of women in the house, just as the exclusive recognition of the natural mother, because of the impossibility of determining the natural father with certainty, signifies high esteem for women, that is, for the mothers. ([1884] 1978:735)

Since what was produced in such societies was shared by everyone, the division of labor between women and men was reciprocal, not exploitative (Guettel 1974:11). Women were viewed as equal and productive members of society, performing domestic labor necessary for the functioning and survival of the group. Their participation in socially valued activities granted them political equality as well, since in communal societies, Engels proposed, those individuals who made decisions also carried them out. The participation of women in a major share of the significant labor needed for society's functioning thus accorded them decision-making power commensurate with their contributions (Leacock 1972:34).

Impact of Private Property on Women

Engels ([1884] 1978) postulated that as the production of wealth increased, private property ownership emerged, and men became more important within the family. They used their strengthened position to overthrow "mother right" and matrilineality in favor of patrilineality and to replace pre-existing marriage forms with monogamous ones. Monogamy was instituted to ensure that a man's wealth and property would be passed on to his own children and to no one else's. This practice was enforced through patriarchal control of the family. Engels claimed that under such conditions, women became degraded, the slaves of men's lust, and mere instruments for breeding children. The movement away from communal ownership and mother right to private property and patriarchy constituted nothing less, according to Engels, than "the world-historical defeat of the female sex" (p. 736).

Women were thus transformed from productive members of society, whose roles as mothers and whose participation in necessary and valued labor had once accorded them social and political equality, into wives dependent on their husbands' activities for survival. Under such circumstances, women's domestic labor was no longer viewed as an important contribution to the larger society. Instead, a woman's labor was seen as work done for her individual family, headed by a man whose role in the outside world granted him power and status. Once women were no longer perceived as important contributors to society's economic functioning, they lost their status as valued members and, with it, their position of political equality. The development of this inequality between men and women, according to Engels, constituted the earliest form of oppression known in human societies. As he phrased it, "The first class antagonism which appears in history coincides with the development of the antagonism between men and women in monogamian marriage and the first class oppression with that of the female sex by the male." (Engels [1884] 1978:739)

Impact of Class Society and the State on Women

With the development of class society, according to Engels, the state arose. In a Marxist perspective, the state is understood as a political mechanism that protects the interests of the elite class. The state does so not only through using political force if need be, but also through the development of institutions that promote an ideology consistent with its interests. An ideology of women's inferiority, many materialist theorists argue, did just that. Thus, with the development of class society, women's status, defined in terms of their equal rights, declined. The new social relations, brought about by an economic pattern based on private property ownership and the accumulation of wealth and supported by state structures, rendered women economically and politically powerless and socially and culturally undervalued, if not disdained.

Influence of Engels' Theory

Engels' model has provided contemporary researchers with a number of areas for further investigation. It has led investigators to ask the following questions:

- Did ancient *matriarchies* or "mother right" societies, in which power was invested in the hands of women, actually ever exist?

- Do women fare better in societies which put them at the center of social organization by tracing descent *matrilineally*?

- What is the relationship between a society's *mode of food production* and sexual stratification?

- How does the existence of *private property* alter women's status?

- What effect does the separation of *public and private spheres*, which accompanies the *rise of state societies*, have on gender oppression?

- Has the spread of *capitalism* around the world had a positive or negative effect on gender inequality?

The next sections in this chapter address each of these questions. They also provide an overview of work undertaken by researchers employing a materialist orientation and reveal the specific strengths and deficiencies of Engels' theoretical formulation.

MATRIARCHIES

Engels drew his knowledge of early communal societies from the work of social evolutionists such as J. J. Bachofen. Using myths as evidence, Bachofen's *Das Mutterrecht* (1861) suggested that women in early societies were unhappy with their promiscuous social order. Revolting against male lust, women instituted a new form of social organization based on the primacy of mother right, which sprang from the natural biological association of mother and child (Bamberger 1974:264). Ultimately, according to Bachofen, men became unhappy with a society based on "nature and sensuality" and revolted, establishing patriarchal rule and subordinating women in the process (Sacks 1980:53). This event produced a superior form of social organization, according to Bachofen, since transcending sensuality allowed men to create the necessary prerequisites of civilization.

Like other social evolutionists, Bachofen ([1861] 1992) proposed the existence of matriarchies somewhere in the West's evolutionary past based on scant evidence. He did so, however, not to praise mother right, as Engels did, but to point to its undesirability. By contrast, many feminists in the 1970s used such accounts much like Engels did, to argue that women in early societies had enjoyed power (see, for example, Leacock 1978). They believed that women's current oppression was best explained in terms of social and economic factors, not in terms of some natural inferiority. Today, assertions of the existence of matriarchal societies have become big business. Book after book claims that mother goddess religions emphasizing fertility are evidence of earlier societies that venerated women, ones in which the "female principle" was in the ascendancy and women had power. Each year New Age shops sell thousands of tiny replicas of what they presume to be fertility idols from mother-right societies in the form of necklaces, earrings, key chains, and T-shirt logos. However, feminist archaeologist Sarah Nelson (1997) has pointed out the problem with interpreting archaeological evidence as indicative of the veneration of women. She suggests that the interpretation of "Venus" figures as ancient fertility symbols is not supported by evidence. Instead, it reproduces a Western male bias. As Nelson puts it, "underlying the description of the figurines as erotic and reproductive is a masculist construction of the world, in which females are assumed to exist primarily for males, sexually or reproductively" (p. 70). Nelson suggests that it is just as likely that the figurines were used as teaching devices for young girls experiencing puberty (p. 71).

Similarly, Joan Bamberger's (1974) analysis of a constellation of myths about "mother rule" from societies in Tierra del Fuego in South America and in the tropical rainforests of the Amazon suggests that these myths do not reveal an actual moment in the past when women had power (also see Murphy and Murphy 1974). To the contrary, she argues that they act to justify male dominance in these societies in the present. The myths begin with a discussion of an earlier time when women ruled and move on to describe a moment when men wrested this control away from them. Men, these stories suggest, needed to do so because women could not handle power or wield it in the proper way— in the way, that is, that men use it today. The myths thus reinforce the properness and desirability of male power. Bamberger concludes her analysis with the following warning: "The myth of matriarchy is but the tool used to keep women bound to her place. To free her, we need to destroy the myth" (1974:280).

Paula Webster concurs with Bamberger that stories about the existence of past matriarchies, whether from our own society or from others, do not represent proof of the actual existence of mother right. Yet, she presents a conclusion that is diametrically opposed to Bamberger's. Webster suggests that the debate over whether matriarchies have ever existed can play an important role in our society:

> It pushes women (and men) to imagine a society that is not patriarchal, one in which women might for the first time have power over their lives. . . . Thus even if feminists reject the existence of matriarchy on empirical and/or theoretical grounds, we should acknowledge the importance of the vision of matriarchy and use the debate for furthering the creation of feminist theory and action. (1975:155–56)

Whether one agrees with Bamberger or with Webster, it seems clear that there is little empirical evidence to substantiate claims that matriarchies ever existed. However, the stories of their existence can act either to oppress women or to offer them a vision of a different world. When claims of ancient mother right are invoked, then, we need to listen carefully to the underlying subtext to decide why the myth of matriarchy is being used. We might ask, for example, whose interest it serves. We might also wish to analyze the role it plays in women's actual lives. Does belief in matriarchy, for example, empower the women who buy "proof" of it from their local New Age stores to take action in the real world against oppression, or does it prevent them from doing so?

MATRILINEALITY

Engels' claim that matrilineality accorded women high esteem in ancient societies has been a source of controversy for many years in anthropology. G. C. Hobhouse (1924), writing in the first decades of the twentieth century, claimed that the position of women is not better in societies with matrilineal descent than in other societies. He argued that women do not necessarily fare better in matrilineal societies because they are still controlled by men, even though these men are their brothers, not their husbands or fathers. Kathleen Gough, by contrast, argues that in matrilineal societies "women tend to have greater independence than in patrilineal societies [even though] the ultimate head of the household lineage and local group is usually a man" (1975:54).

How Matrilineality Works

To understand these seemingly contradictory statements, it is necessary to see how *matrilineal descent systems* work. In a matrilineal society, people's relatives are not determined by tracing relationships through both one's mother and father, as they are in the mainstream culture of many Western societies. This system of reckoning kinship is known as bilateral ("two sides") descent. In contrast, in unilineal systems, whether patrilineal or matrilineal, relationships are traced through one parent's side only. In patrilineal societies the father's line is emphasized, while in matrilineal societies, the mother's line is used. In unilineal systems one's social identity; access to resources; and rights, duties, and obligations are defined by membership in a descent group.

In a matrilineal society, one's descent group would consist of all members related to a person through connections with a woman. If you lived in such a society, some of the individuals who would belong to your matrilineage would include your mother, her mother, your brothers and sisters (you share a mother with them), your mother's brothers and sisters (they share a mother with your mother), and your mother's sisters' children (their mother and your mother share a mother). Many people whom you think of as your relatives if you trace descent bilaterally would not be considered members of your descent group in a matrilineal society. These individuals would include your father and grandfather (your father belongs to his mother's group and his father to his mother's group), your mother's brothers' children (they belong to the matrilineage of their mother), and your mother's father (he, too, belongs to his mother's group).

As you can see, while a woman's father and husband are not part of her matrilineage, her brothers are. Under such circumstances, men typically show stronger loyalty toward their mothers and sisters than to their wives (Nielsen 1990:33). Yet a man frequently lives with his wife's family in a matrilineal society, a circumstance that can potentially give rise to conflicting duties and responsibilities. This situation can be attenuated somewhat by granting authority over women and children to a woman's brother (Nielsen 1990:33). This clarification should help explain Hobhouse's and Gough's seemingly contradictory statements.

Just because women are the links in a matrilineal kinship system does not necessarily mean that they wield power and authority. Their brothers might instead.

Domestic Authority in Matrilineal Societies

To investigate the role male authority plays in matrilineal societies, Alice Schlegel (1972) constructed a continuum of matrilineal societies based on who wields authority in a woman's household. On one side of the continuum were societies in which brothers had total control over women, while on the other side were those in which husbands did. She found that at both ends of the continuum, women had little independence and little freedom to make their own decisions. In societies falling between the two extremes, where brothers and husbands shared domestic authority equally, however, women's autonomy was much greater. This finding led Schlegel to conclude that domestic power declines as it disperses. The implication of Schlegel's study is that tracing descent through females alone does not guarantee women a high degree of autonomy. Instead, it is the pattern of domestic power relations in such societies that affects women's options.

Impact of Matrilineality on Women

Martin K. Whyte (1978) analyzed the relationship of matrilineality to women's position in society. His analysis, like Schlegel's, suggests that it is too simple to claim that women have a high status in such societies. He argues that we need to uncover the specific benefits of matrilineality for women. His cross-cultural analysis reveals that matrilineality is associated with several advantages for women, including a greater control by women over property, greater domestic authority, and a higher value placed on their lives (p. 133).

No recent study confirms Engels' claim that in matrilineal societies women necessarily enjoy a higher position than women do in other types of societies. Instead, these studies suggest that matrilineality may confer some specific advantages to women and that the particular type of domestic arrangement may be more important in influencing the extent of women's freedom and independence.

Patrilineality and Women's Negotiations

While women generally have more advantages in matrilineal societies than in patrilineal ones, this does not mean they are without any power and control within all patrilineal societies. Gaining power can occur through playing a particular role within those societies. For example, in Taiwan, where a powerful bond exists between mothers and sons, a wife is often subjugated to her husband and his mother. When she has sons of her own, however, and becomes a mother-in-law herself, she is able to wield considerable power and attain a high status within the household (Wolf 1972).

Among the Nandi of Kenya, a patrilineal people who practice a mixed economy of herding and farming, a woman can raise her status by marrying another woman. According to Nandi ideology, men must manage the most important property: livestock and land (Oboler 1993:136). When a woman marries, she acquires rights to some of her husband's property, which she will pass on to her sons. For a woman with no sons, this situation presents a problem. She will be unable to pass down her property unless she opts either to adopt a male child, to stay in her natal household, to have her husband control her property, or to become a female husband. In this latter case, the woman takes another woman in marriage who will bear her sons (through impregnation by a man, of course). The female husband, who also may have a male husband (see Oboler 1993:139), has all the non-sexual prerogatives of a male husband in regard to his wife, and she also acquires other rights associated with being a man, such as the right to manage family property and to exercise legitimate authority over children. This increases the woman's status significantly in this male-dominated society (Oboler 1993:138–39).

Women-Centered Kinship Networks

Other researchers have focused on kinship, power, and the economy to reveal how women work within the confines of particular kinship systems to create options that grant them social power and economic flexibility. Unlike Engels, these researchers are not primarily concerned with explaining women's status. Instead, they treat women as social actors and show how power and position are not allocated in fixed ways, but how they can be manipulated by women to increase their position, control, and power, and to cope with economic circumstances. Since, as Shirley Lindenbaum claims, "relations of kinship are in certain societies, relations of production" (quoted in Brettell and Sargent 1993:318), kinship continues to be an important factor to consider in accounts of gender asymmetry.

Using an interactionist approach, Carol Stack (1974) has found that among African Americans living in poverty in the U.S. Midwest, women create women-centered families that are bound together by female kinship and friendships. These networks provide women with economic and emotional support. Such kinship connections create a network of relationships within which women exchange goods and services and cope in the face of harsh conditions. Women-centered households are fairly common. For example, they can be found in the Dominican Republic (Brown 1975), among sectors of the British working class (Morpeth and Langton 1973), and among Japanese-Americans (Yanagisako 1977).

Micaela di Leonardo (1997) has also found similar kinship networks among Italian-American women in northern California. Her
analysis reveals the extent to which women are involved in initiating,
maintaining, and celebrating cross-household kinship ties through such
devices as visiting, telephoning, sending cards and presents, and organizing holiday events (p. 341). She found that while such "kin work" is
unpaid labor for women and is sometimes viewed as a burden, it is also
a source of satisfaction for women and a route for attaining power not
available to them in the labor market (p. 347).

MODES OF FOOD PRODUCTION

Engels' model is based on the assumption that in pre-class societies women's role in subsistence activities provided the basic necessities
of life, ensuring them equal status with men. He asserts that women
performed activities compatible with their reproductive functions, while
men undertook other necessary tasks. This sexual division of labor, however, was not exploitative, since both men and women performed tasks
necessary for the group's survival.

This assertion has led many anthropologists to focus on the role
that the sexual division of labor plays in societies with different subsistence strategies, or modes of production. These modes include foraging
(hunter-gatherer) societies in which food is obtained by hunting animals
and gathering fruits and vegetables; horticultural societies that practice small-scale cultivation of plants based on the use of the hoe; pastoral societies that depend primarily on herd-animal husbandry; and
agrarian societies that usually employ the plow in cultivation and use
irrigation systems and fertilizers to increase yields. These subsistence
strategies are also used in combination in some societies.

Foraging or Hunter-Gatherer Societies

There is little stratification in foraging societies of any kind, which
is most likely related to the difficulty of building a surplus in a society
that does not produce its own food. There is almost no private property
ownership either. In general, in such societies, women enjoy an equal
position with men, although certain exceptions do exist.

Among foragers, there is no universal form of division of labor by
sex. As we have seen, early studies assumed that women were the gath-
erers and men the hunters in such societies. Subsequent research has
shown, however, that there is great variation in the subsistence tasks
undertaken by men and women in different foraging societies. Among
the Mbuti of the Ituri forest, for example, women along with men play

an active role in the capture of animals in nets (Duffy 1996), while among the Tiwi of Australia, men forage for some foodstuffs while women forage for others (Goodale [1971] 1994). In most foraging societies, women contribute the bulk of subsistence foods, sometimes as much as 75 percent. Women's contribution to subsistence is, for the most part, related to a high status for women in foraging societies. In an analysis drawing on Engels, Eleanor Leacock (1978) suggests that this status is due to several factors. Women's work in foraging societies contributes to the overall group, and there is no division in such societies between a public and a private sphere with men relegated to the first and women to the second. In addition, individuals who carry out decisions tend to make them. These factors, according to Leacock, grant women a great deal of autonomy within foraging societies.

Horticultural Societies

Among horticulturists, women continue to play an active role in subsistence, although their contributions do not necessarily result in high status. This finding suggests that women's contribution to subsistence alone cannot account for their position within society. According to Joyce Nielsen (1990), kinship organization within horticultural societies is more significant for determining women's position than their subsistence contribution. In line with researchers discussed earlier in this chapter, Nielsen suggests that the presence of matrilineality is the significant factor influencing women's lives in horticultural societies (pp. 32–36). However, she also points out that there is variation in women's position in horticultural societies that practice matrilineal descent, suggesting this variation can be explained by differing residence rules that govern where or with whom a couple is expected to live after marriage (p. 29).

In matrilineal societies, two types of residence patterns dominate: *matrilocal* residence, in which a newly married couple lives with or near the bride's family, and *avunculocal* residence, in which the couple lives with or near the husband's maternal uncle. This latter pattern should make sense, given the previous discussion of the importance of a woman's brother to her and thus to her children in matrilineal societies. In societies that practice matrilineal descent, Nielsen (1990) argues, women fare better in those with matrilocal residence than in those with avunculocal residence. With matrilocal residence, related women are kept together while men are dispersed, discouraging concentrated male power. With avunculocal residence, however, it is women who are dispersed. Drawing on the work of Kay Martin and Barbara Voorhies (1975), Nielsen suggests that matrilocal residence is found in horticultural societies in which food sources are abundant; there is little competition over resources decreasing the threat of warfare; and there is no surplus production. Under such circumstances, related men need not be kept together (Nielsen 1990:33).

In societies with avunculocal residence, a woman is a member of a household in which the distribution of land and products is controlled by a man unrelated to her (usually her husband's maternal uncle). She will, thus, have less autonomy in decision-making opportunities and will be less valued by the group than if she resides with members of her own descent group. Thus, according to this analysis, subsistence contributions alone do not account for women's position in horticultural societies. Their status is mediated by kinship structures and residence rules.

Pastoral Societies

Pastoral societies involve animal herding and are noted for the importance placed on men. They are almost always patrilineal, patrilocal (a newly married couple goes to live with or near the husband's family), and patriarchal. Women's contribution to subsistence is frequently low in these societies, although studies of some East African groups report that women occasionally herd large animals and perform tasks related to the maintenance of animals, such as watering, feeding, milking, and caring for young livestock (Dahl 1987). The combination of patrilocal residence pattern and a strict division of labor, not surprisingly, leads to a relatively low status for women in most pastoral societies, although there are many exceptions.

Agricultural Societies

Several authors claim that the rise of plow agriculture corresponds to a decline in women's position due to the loss of their productive role. Martin and Voorhies (1975) suggest that with the adoption of intensive cultivation techniques, especially the use of the plow and irrigation, a sexual division of labor develops in which men usurp women's position as primary producers. This change in women's productive tasks occurs, they argue, because such innovations require strength and prolonged absences from the household, a requirement incompatible with child rearing (see Brown 1970). Consequently, women are withdrawn from agricultural production and become isolated in the domestic realm where they are concerned primarily with childcare. At the same time, ideologies develop to justify women's domestic isolation. According to Martin and Voorhies:

> The economic horizons of women are thereby gradually limited to the physical and social space of the domicile. Entirely new mythologies appear to redefine the innate aptitudes of the sexes with respect to domestic and extradomestic horizons. (1975:331)

Substantiating this claim is Matthiasson's (1974) finding that there is a relationship between women's participation in agriculture and public status. In societies in which women are heavily involved in agricultural production, such as in the Philippines and Cambodia, the status of women is high. In places in which women participate little in such activities, as among the peasants of China, North and Central India, and Egypt, men tend to dominate public life (p. 433).

Ester Boserup (1970) has pointed to the detrimental effects of the adoption of plow agriculture on women's position in societies that have been affected by colonial practices. According to her research, due to population pressures on foraging groups, some societies adopted horticulture with shifting cultivation. Under such conditions, it was common for women to engage in more horticultural work than men and to enjoy a considerable degree of autonomy as well. However, with even greater population pressures, plow agriculture emerged, and with it, women lost their productive role. This change was primarily the result of colonial policies that encouraged men to take over farming by introducing cash crops and new farming technologies exclusively through men (see Quinn 1977:185).

According to Martin and Voorhies, the effect of colonial introduction of agricultural techniques on women's role and status is also mediated by kinship structures. Colonial practices, which favored men's participation in agricultural labor, also encouraged the development of the nuclear family, which acted to isolate women from a larger social group. Furthermore, according to them:

> Colonial administrators and missionaries took the initiative in inculcating European institutions and value systems. Since the culture they brought with them had a strong patriarchal base, the social and economic horizons of the colonized male were characteristically broadened at the expense of women. (Martin and Voorhies 1975:297)

Women's Contribution to Subsistence

This review suggests that while women's contribution to subsistence does not necessarily guarantee high status, it seems to be a prerequisite for it. Women tend to fare better in foraging and horticultural societies where their labor is significant to the group's basic needs than they do in pastoral and agrarian ones, although their higher position may also be related to the general lack of stratification in general among foragers and horticulturists.

PRIVATE PROPERTY

Engels ([1884] 1978) contended that with the emergence of private property and the rise of the state, women were relegated to the domestic sphere and reduced to a position of dependence and subservience. Several authors have expanded on this assertion, and, in the process, have offered important qualifications of Engels' position.

Martin K. Whyte (1978) has tested the hypothesis that women have lower status in societies possessing significant private property rights to the means of production. His cross-cultural analysis suggests that the only strong relationship existing between private property and women's position is that in societies with private property, women's labor tends to be less valued than in those societies without it. Interestingly, Whyte has also found that women tend to have more informal influence in societies with private property, leading him to conclude:

> There may be a modest tendency in cultures with private property for women to have somewhat lower status or more restricted roles in some areas of social life than in other cultures. The figures . . . do not lead us to believe, however, that the advantage of private property is in some sense the crucial change affecting women. (1978:38)

Furthermore, Whyte suggests that the existence of private property cannot itself explain why men take control of it in the first place, an assumption underlying Engels' analysis. Christine Gailey (1998:47–48) has raised a similar criticism. She calls into question Engels' assumption that there is a necessary relationship between private property and a desire on the part of men to transmit property to their biological children.

PUBLIC/PRIVATE SPHERES IN STATE SOCIETIES

Rayna (Rapp) Reiter (1975c) focuses on the implications for women of the split between public and private realms that accompanies the development of the state. She argues that when states arose, kin groups lost their role as determiners of access to important societal resources. Instead, access was decided by membership in the class that consolidated control. Under such conditions, the elite class, whose interests the state serves, developed a monopoly on force, not only to control and defend its territory, but also to ensure its access to people's labor (in the form of taxes or the military draft, for example). But the use of repressive force is not a practical way to guarantee conformity. It is more effective to convince people through ideological mechanisms of the value of their compliance.

One mechanism that enabled state control over people's minds, according to Reiter, was the separation of the public and private spheres of life. Superstructual institutions, such as educational and religious systems, perpetuated the view that work in the public sphere was valuable, but not in the private sphere. It did so by inculcating the idea that labor in the public sphere was for the good of the state and thus for the good of all. By contrast, the work of the people who labored in the private sphere was seen to benefit only individual families. Because of women's roles in childbearing and child rearing, Reiter argues, they are confined to the domestic sphere in class societies, while men participate in public activities. Thus, in state societies, the power and prestige associated with the private domain is extremely limited, and women's work within it is highly devalued (for other analyses of the importance of the public/private split, see Sacks 1974 and 1980 and Sanday 1981).

CRITIQUE OF THE PUBLIC/PRIVATE DICHOTOMY

The significance of the distinction between public and private realms and the importance of the rise of the state for women's position have been debated in the anthropological literature for some time. From the perspective of the 1990s, it is easy to see how North American women's fight for equal access to the public sphere of work in the 1970s influenced theorists like the ones discussed above. However, as Louise Lamphere (1997:84) suggests, "as appealing as this dichotomy [between public and private spheres] seemed in the abstract, it turned out to be difficult to apply when actually looking at examples of women's activities in other cultures." She feels that even in societies in which there is a clear association of men with the public sphere and women with the private, and powerful ideologies validating this distinction, these dichotomies are never quite that neatly arranged in actuality.

Another criticism of the validity of this distinction has come from women of color. Aida Hurtado, for example, has argued:

> Women of Color have never had the benefit of the economic conditions that underlie the public/private distinction. . . . Welfare programs and policies have discouraged family life, sterilization programs have restricted reproduction rights, government has drafted and armed disproportionate numbers of people of Color to fight its wars overseas, police forces and the criminal justice system arrest and incarcerate disproportionate numbers of people of Color. There is no such thing as a private sphere for people of Color except that

which they manage to create and protect in an otherwise hostile environment. (1989:849)

Nonetheless, Lamphere (1997) reminds us that this public/private dichotomy has been useful in showing how an ideology of "women's place is in the home" has operated in such countries as the United States, Great Britain, and France, the very kinds of societies Engels focused on in his analysis of oppression in industrialized capitalist states (p. 86). The focus on the division between the public and private spheres has highlighted the importance of women's work within the domestic realm and has illuminated the significant role it plays in the overall functioning of capitalist societies, even though that work is unpaid. Emphasis on public/private spheres in the 1970s also led many people in North America to question the consequences of men's traditional lack of contribution to the domestic realm and to call for more equal participation by men in household duties and child-care responsibilities (see Rosaldo 1974). As a result, many men in the last two decades have experienced a higher-quality relationship with their wives and children.

While questions about the rise of the state and its impact on women and the links between class oppression and gender oppression are still central to feminist anthropology, work has moved away from Engels' focus on the evolutionary development of the state. This focus, critics argue, has produced an inaccurate notion of the state as a singular entity. As Caroline Brettell and Carolyn Sargent put it, universal evolutionary paradigms like Engels' "that posit a uniform impact of the rise of the state on gender roles cannot do justice to the myriad ways in which specific cultural histories, diverse social hierarchies, and systems of stratification affect gender relations and ideology" (1997:262).

As feminist theorizing of the state has expanded since the 1970s, the focus has, indeed, shifted away from making claims about *the state* to an attempt to understand the variety of state approaches to the institutionalization of gender relations. This approach has also moved researchers away from a focus on "women" toward a concentration on the ways in which specific groups of women are affected by a particular nation's state policies (Ferree, Lorber, and Hess 1999:xxiii).

Studies by feminist archaeologists have been particularly fruitful in revealing the variation in women's position under different state formations. Freidel and Schele (1997) have shown, for example, that among the lowland Maya of the Yucatan peninsula in the Classic Period (A.D 300 to A.D. 900), royal women could play a significant role in the politics of the state, ruling along with men "in the context of court politics revolving around family alliances and feuds" (p. 75).

CAPITALISM

Marx and Engels' work has also been a starting point for many researchers interested in the emergence of a global economy and its impact on women. These studies have tended to focus on the effects wrought by capitalism's exportation around the world. Capitalism as a broad category, and its impact on "developing" nations, has been identified as having profound and detrimental effects on women's roles and position.

Early studies of this kind tended to focus on how the position of women in Third World nations was affected adversely by an international exchange system that placed developing nations in a position of dependency on First World nations. The term "Third World" refers to a loose category of approximately 120 countries that are dependent technologically on highly industrialized, relatively affluent "First World" nations. Third World or developing countries are characterized by high population growth and low standards of living. A small, wealthy elite usually controls much of the nation's economy.

Dependency theory asserts that economic development occurs in the context of an international economic system that extracts wealth from developing nations and transforms their economies in order to support the needs of "advanced" capitalist countries (Bossen 1984:4). Dependent development creates an international division of labor in which Third World countries must respond to the demands of industrialized capitalist societies. It also intensifies the sexual division of labor since, under such circumstances, men tend to be integrated into formal capitalist work relations while women are relegated to pre-capitalist or domestic work, toiling in the home without pay to reproduce and maintain a labor force (see Harrison 1991; Nash and Safa 1980). The introduction of this new division of labor, according to Laurel Bossen (1984), is accomplished by extolling women's reproductive roles while disparaging their productive ones. The advantage to a capitalist economy of this relegation of women to the home is that it provides a reserve labor supply, one that can be called upon to offset the demands of men for higher wages.

While Engels' theory, as we have seen, understands power relations between men and women within the context of different modes of production, dependency theory broadens the context to include a consideration of how the international economy affects women's opportunities under particular conditions. For example, researchers interested in this larger context have revealed how, among the Lesotho of Africa, mining draws men away from their villages. This situation leaves women who are left behind with more opportunity to participate in community life (Meuller 1977), although it also leaves them with more work to perform.

Ann Stoler (1977) has documented a similar circumstance in colonial Indonesia. She shows how its labor-intensive sugar plantation economy pulled both men and women into the labor force. More recent studies have shown that women need to control strategic resources in capitalist societies in order to maintain their status and power both at home and in the larger community (Brettell and Sargent 1997:468).

THE GLOBAL ECONOMY

The effect of women's employment in multinational corporations has provided an important focus for recent investigation of the effect of capitalist penetration on women around the world. In many countries women make up a disproportionate number of the labor force in such employment, especially in "high-tech" manufacturing plants. The appeal of women as workers to multinational employers in many Third World countries has been attributed to their traditional socialization and training. As Brydon and Chant put it:

> Women's socialization, training in needlework, embroidery and other domestic crafts, and supposedly "natural" aptitude for detailed handiwork, gives them an advantage over men in tasks requiring high levels of manual dexterity and accuracy; women are also supposedly more passive—willing to accept authority and less likely to become involved in labour conflicts. Finally, women have the added advantage of "natural disposability"—when they leave to get married to have children, a factory temporarily cutting back on production simply freezes their post. (quoted in Brettell and Sargent 1997:469)

The effect such employment has on women is controversial. Some focus on the financial stability it grants women while others "see multinationals perpetuating or even creating new forms of inequality as they introduce young women to a new set of individualist and consumer values" (Brettell and Sargent 1997:469). In general, most researchers agree that women's employment in multinational corporations in non-Western countries has been exploitative; women are often brutally overworked and underpaid (see Ong 1987). When globalization results in the development of tourism as a Third World country's primary industry, the effects can be devastating. In Thailand, for example, "sex tourism" has become big business. Men travel from around the world to have sexual access to "exotic" women who are often housed in unbearable living quarters and threatened every day by the possibility of contracting AIDS.

CONCLUSIONS

It should be clear from this review that Engels' work has had a lasting influence on studies by anthropologists interested in gender and sexual stratification. While the research reviewed in this chapter has also gone far to qualify and revise some of his assertions, it all shares with Engels' work, to a greater or lesser extent, a basic premise that is the hallmark of a materialist theoretical orientation. This assumption is that the techno-economic order of a society is the prime mover in establishing all other forms of social relations. This understanding helps explain why, for example, ideas about men's superior worth have arisen in class societies like those of the United States and Canada. Men's wage labor directly benefited capitalist owners of factories and corporations, while women's work in the home only indirectly did so. With the advent of the women's movement, more and more women moved into the public sphere of employment, yet the underevaluation of women's domestic labor carried over. Women were shunted into jobs that were seen as extensions of their domestic role, such as nursing, teaching, and daycare providers. While the media make much of the opportunities opened to women since the 1970s, in actuality, women are still crowded into a few occupations that are seen as appropriately female. Men, by contrast, have a much wider range of occupational opportunities from which to chose. According to Nielsen, in the United States, 50 percent of all employed women work in fewer than 50 different occupations that are at least 80 percent female while over half of all men work in 229 occupations that are at least 80 percent male (1990:12). Moreover, the occupations that are associated with traditional women's work continue to be seen as less significant to society, a fact reflected in the lower pay and prestige associated with these forms of employment.

But do material factors explain all aspects of stratification? While it is difficult to deny the crucial importance of economic factors on people's lives, the relative causal weight that can be given to them is an open and highly debated question. Speaking broadly, Marx and Engels contended that the economic base of a society determined its political, social, and cultural institutions. The materialist approach, in general, understands ideological factors, which influence gender constructions and systems of oppression, as the superstructural expressions of the underlying material base of a society. In other words, ideas are seen as reflections of the interests of the ruling or elite class, instilled in members of a society in the contemporary world through such institutions as schools, churches, and the media. This reduction of ideology to class interest largely ignores the independent existence of such factors as race and ethnicity in affecting a person's social position or life chances. While some would argue that race and ethnicity are merely ideological constructs used to maintain the interests of a largely white, Anglo-Saxon class of owners, others contend that class alone cannot explain racism and ethnic prejudice.

A similar argument has been made about gender. Many researchers claim that materialist explanations cannot account for women's secondary position to men in most societies, a circumstance that they argue exists regardless of a society's underlying economic structures or whether classes exist or not. It is to these kinds of arguments that we turn in the next chapter.

Chapter Six

Structuralist Approaches

The theories discussed in this and the next chapter emphasize the ideas that members of a society hold and analyze the way these ideas are represented in language, myths, or symbols. Unlike materialist theorists, anthropologists who take such an *ideational* approach reject the premise that the material conditions of life determine other aspects of social organization. They view the ideational realm of culture not as a superstructural outgrowth of underlying economic relations as materialists do but as having an independent reality. Ideas are understood as distinct and autonomous factors that not only exert an influence over the behavior of individuals but also constitute an individual's very sense of self.

The purpose of this chapter is to introduce you to ideational approaches to gender by using the ideas of the French anthropologist Claude Lévi-Strauss as a starting point. Our aim is to focus on *structuralism*, the particular ideational approach associated with Lévi-Strauss, to give you an indepth understanding of one influential ideational approach to gender studies and to assess the strengths and limitations of this approach.

IDEATIONAL APPROACHES TO GENDER

The roots of the ideational approach in anthropology go back to the late nineteenth and early twentieth centuries and can be found in the works of American anthropologist Franz Boas and French sociologist Émile Durkheim. One of the most influential strands of this approach for explaining gender relations and sexual asymmetry, however, did not emerge in anthropology until the mid-twentieth century with the publication in English of Lévi-Strauss' *The Elementary Structures of Kinship*

(1969). Lévi-Strauss' structuralist approach focused not only on the importance of ideas but also on how the mind is structured to organize them. According to Lévi-Strauss, myths, rituals, and even aspects of social organization, such as kinship systems, can be understood to be like language. All are reflections of the underlying structure of the human brain. This structure, according to Lévi-Strauss, is binary: all human thought is dualistic, dividing the world into sets of oppositional categories like black and white, male and female, and nature and culture. Lévi-Strauss viewed cultural expressions like myth and kinship as cognitive efforts to resolve fundamental paradoxes set up by such binary categorizations. One such paradox, according to Lévi-Strauss, is the one produced by the recognition that humans are both natural (animals) and cultural. While Lévi-Strauss drew on linguistic models in his analyses and focused on symbolic systems, he also assumed that biological structures in the brain explain cultural forms.

Lévi-Strauss' ideas had an important impact on feminist anthropologists writing in the 1970s, especially on Sherry Ortner (1974), whose article "Is Female to Male as Nature Is to Culture?" is now considered a classic in feminist studies. In it, Ortner drew heavily on Lévi-Strauss' work to explain what she assumed were women's devaluation and subordination in all societies. Ortner integrated structuralist assumptions with the ideas of the French writer and philosopher, Simone de Beauvoir, who is best known for her claim in *The Second Sex* that "woman is not born, but made" (1953). This phrase summarizes Beauvoir's understanding of gender as a cultural construct—as the meaning given to the physical or biological traits that differentiate males and females. Beauvoir's influence on Ortner, as well as on many other feminist writers, lies in her focus on the role that Western categories like male and female, Self and Other play in women's subordination and on how ideas about the body are related to notions about who a person is or can be.

As we have seen, biosocial theorists argue that women's bodily functions predispose them to particular gender roles and behaviors, which, in turn, give rise to a sexual division of labor and women's position in society. As discussed earlier, these investigators focus on the "naturalness" of such outcomes, claiming that they have resulted from evolutionary processes having to do with the survival of our species. Beauvoir, by contrast, argued that if women's bodies have constrained them, it is because women have been interpreted through the lens of culture, thought of as "natural" by men who have created the very category of "nature" to serve their own aims.

Many recent writers have followed Beauvoir's lead and have analyzed how cultural constructions of women's bodies continue to affect women's lives. Some of these analyses show how such constructions of the female body can have devastating effects on women, while others focus on how women work within the constraints of these representations to construct identities that manipulate and refuse cultural norms. Still other researchers have gone beyond structuralist approaches and draw on what is called post-structuralist ideas. We discuss these newer approaches in chapter 7.

LÉVI-STRAUSS' STRUCTURALIST MODEL

The basic aim of the structuralist theoretical orientation is to uncover the universal, essential structure of the human mind. Because of this goal, Lévi-Strauss focused his efforts on uncovering the logic behind such quintessentially human inventions as art, myth, and social organization. According to Lévi-Strauss, the human mind works the same way everywhere because the human brain is structured the same way everywhere.

Binary Opposition and Meaning

Lévi-Strauss drew his understanding of the particular form that thinking takes from linguist Ferdinand de Saussure, who claimed that language is a system that creates meaning by setting up binary oppositions between signs or sounds. For example, the word "vat" differs from the word "bat" by only one sound. Thus, in English, the sound associated with the letter or sign "b" carries meaning, just as the sound associated with the letter or sign "v" does. The meaning of the word "vat" is different from the meaning of the word "bat" because "b" is not "v" and "v" is not "b." Thus meaning has been constructed through opposing "b" with "v."

In discovering this system, Saussure felt he had discovered the deep structure of language and the underlying law governing it: meaning is produced through setting up oppositions between signs. Speakers of a language, however, are not necessarily conscious of this process; they need not know how the underlying structure of language produces meaning in order to speak it.

Drawing on Saussure, Lévi-Strauss claimed that the underlying structure of myths and kinship systems can also be explained in terms of this particular logical structure, even though this structure is not conscious. He sought to show how social institutions can be analyzed in terms of the binary oppositions that the mind sets up. At the same time, he pointed to the problem inherent in all binary oppositions: they are arbitrary. Lévi-Strauss contended that, at some level, the mind recognizes this flaw and is dissatisfied. It knows that the binary oppositions it has established are not real but are the product of how the mind operates. To remedy this situation the mind produces signs or symbols that mediate between oppositions. These mediators, in essence, act as in-between categories, ones that have characteristics of both of the original binary categories.

To understand Lévi-Strauss's model of how the mind works, think of a traffic light. It works on the basis of opposing colors. The human mind breaks the light spectrum, which is actually continuous, into discrete categories that are then identified as particular colors. In the traffic signal, colors are used to set up a binary opposition between two signs that are then mediated by a third sign. Red is a sign carrying the meaning "stop," while green is a sign carrying the meaning "go." But there is no natural association of red with stopping and green with going. Nor is there only one way to divide the light spectrum into discrete and particular categories of color. This arbitrariness requires the binary opposition set up between stop and go to be mediated by a third term, the yellow light. The meaning of yellow in this system of signs is neither go nor stop but something in between the two. It means "slow down" and "be cautious" (this, at least, is the legal meaning of the yellow light; we all know that some drivers interpret this sign as "speed up"). The yellow light, in structuralist terms, mediates between stop and go.

What does this have to do with gender and sexual asymmetry? As you will see, according to Lévi-Strauss, it has to do with the origin of marriage in which women become signs in a system of meaning. As signs, women are exchanged between groups of men in order to create alliances between them. Creating such bonds arises out of the need of humans to transcend nature and to come together into groups that are orderly and structured.

Nature/Culture and the Incest Taboo

According to Lévi-Strauss, the categories "nature" and "culture" are a pair of binary oppositions that the human mind develops to organize the world. We know something is natural because it does not belong to the category "culture," and we know something is cultural because it does not belong to the category "nature." What about humans who are at once natural and cultural? This logical paradox, according to Lévi-Strauss, is solved by the development of an incest taboo, which is a supposedly universal law that prohibits mating with close kin. The incest taboo works to overcome the randomness of mating found in nature by establishing orderly kinship relations required for cultures to function (Murphy 1971:199). It is a mediator between the categories "nature" and "culture," because it allows the natural act of mating to continue, but in a way that is regulated by culture. The incest taboo functions to define the categories into which one can and cannot mate, thereby forming the basis for marriage rules in all societies. These rules of exogamy

extend the incest taboo by requiring individuals to find marriage partners from outside their social group. For Lévi-Strauss, the development
of the incest taboo marks the critical transition of humans from nature
to culture and is at the foundation of all social organization.

Marriage and the Exchange of Women

Lévi-Strauss (1971) asserted that what is essential about marriage is that it is governed by rules that call for the reciprocal exchange
of women by men. This exchange creates alliances among biologically
unrelated groups of individuals so that society can be formed (p. 355).
As with language, which enables communication through an exchange
of signs, marriage enables relationships among social groups through
an exchange of signs, that is, through the exchange of women. The universal incest taboo ensures that

> the risk of seeing a biological family become established as a closed
> system is definitely eliminated; the biological group can no longer
> stand apart and the bond of alliance with another family ensures
> that dominance of the social over the biological, and the cultural over
> the natural. (Lévi-Strauss 1971:355)

Lévi-Strauss argues that women are the objects of exchange that
cement group affiliation because they can fulfill the biological sexual
urges of men. Because the male sex drive, unlike other "instincts," can
be delayed, a network of relationships based on the anticipation of even-
tual gratification can arise. A system of generalized reciprocity thus
develops in which a man from one family gives a daughter in marriage
to a man in another family with the expectation that yet another family,
sometime in the future, will provide a daughter for one of his sons to
marry. Women are thus the gifts exchanged among men to cement relationships and ensure group cohesion, much as in many societies gifts
are exchanged at Christmas between different families to facilitate the
continuation of a social relationship into the future.

Since it is men who exchange women, at least according to Lévi-
Strauss, it is men who are the beneficiaries of the exchange. Since
women are for men to exchange, they are in no position to give themselves away (Rubin 1975:175). Women are objects in this system—
things to be exchanged. Men are subjects—people who are able to act on
their own volition.

Marriage and the Sexual Division of Labor

According to Lévi-Strauss, in order for marriage and kinship systems to operate there must be interdependence between the sexes so that
the union of man and woman will take place. This interdependence arises
from the sexual division of labor, which is found in all societies. This divi-

sion classifies tasks into those that can be performed by men and those by women. Men and women must, therefore, depend on one another since each is incapable of doing all the tasks necessary for survival. Since the particular tasks allotted to each sex vary across cultures,

> it is the mere fact of [the sexual division of labor's] existence which is mysteriously required, the form under which it comes to exist being utterly irrelevant, at least from the point of view of any natural necessity . . . the sexual division of labor is nothing else than a device to institute a reciprocal state of dependency between the sexes. (Lévi-Strauss 1971:347–48)

The oppression of women, according to Lévi-Strauss' structuralist model, arises from the nature of all social systems that must use women as objects to cement social relationships. Since humans became cultural by instituting an incest taboo that initiates this exchange, women's subordination is synonymous with the very emergence of human beings. In summary, to be human, women are required to be subordinate while men are social initiators, even though there is interdependence between the sexes in the division of labor.

CRITIQUE OF LÉVI-STRAUSS

Lévi-Strauss explained the universal subordination of women not through invoking biological factors per se but through focusing on the cultural interpretations of biological attributes. He assumed that the explanation for women's secondary status in all societies is due to universal cognitive processes. According to him, stereotypes about males and females are not based on the needs of specific social systems but on the common need of all humans to mediate the transition from nature to culture. As Ortner states, for Lévi-Strauss and for herself: "Local variables of economy, ecology, history, political and social structure, values and worldview . . . could explain variation within the universal, but they could not explain the universal itself" (1974:83).

For Lévi-Strauss, women's universal subordination is grounded in the role women play as signs in a system of exchange. Men are more highly valued than women, not because of some innate superiority that is genetically grounded or based on some physical characteristic such as speed or strength, but because of the very way the human mind organizes the world into opposing categories.

Several problematic assumptions lie at the base of this structuralist argument, many of which have not been substantiated by data. For example, there is no evidence that people at all times and in all places think through the construction of binary oppositions. Since Western thinking has been based on such oppositions, some have accused Lévi-Strauss of ethnocentrism: projecting Western ideas on to all other human beings.

Lévi-Strauss' ethnocentrism, according to one of his critics, Carol MacCormack, is also apparent in his assumption that there is a universal human need to transcend nature. Drawing on the work of Marshall Sahlins, she argues that the idea that humans have developed out of a state of nature is the origin myth of Western capitalism. The opposed categories of nature and culture, according to her, are historically specific, not universal. Their opposition can be traced to a specific time and place: eighteenth-century Europe (MacCormack 1980:7). However, while the nature/culture dichotomy may not be universal, Michael Peletz (1996) has recently suggested that this concept may not be confined to Western thinking. Peletz argues that the association of women with animality and men with reason in Islamic societies may date back to a period before the eighteenth century, which suggests that there is still work to be done to clarify the roots of such gender constructs.

Lévi-Strauss' analysis has also been criticized for its assumption that kinship systems are dependent upon women being circulated as objects in a network of exchange. The assertion that it is men who must necessarily be in control of an exchange of women neglects evidence to the contrary. According to Gayle Rubin, "Kinship systems do not merely exchange women, they exchange sexual access, genealogical standing, lineage names, and ancestors, rights and people—men, women, and children—in concrete systems of social relations" (1975:177). Only if the active role of women in kinship structures is denied can Lévi-Strauss' formulation be given credence.

ORTNER'S STRUCTURALIST MODEL

To explain why women are considered inferior to men in all societies, Sherry Ortner (1974) expands Lévi-Strauss' conceptualization of women's oppression and draws from Beauvoir's conclusions that men's creative abilities contribute to their superiority over women. Women's inferiority, according to Ortner, cannot be due to what women actually contribute to society, because what women do in all societies is significant to the overall maintenance and perpetuation of the social group. Why, then, she asks, are women always thought of as inferior? Why are they so often associated with what is defiling? Why are they always excluded from the highest forms of power?

Women as Closer to Nature

Ortner (1974) argues that it is women's association with nature in all societies that gives rise to the universal evaluation of women as inferior to men. According to her, this categorization occurs because a woman's body and its functions are involved more of the time than men's with "species life," with giving birth to, and caring for, children. Women are placed closer to the physical world and thus closer to nature. According to Ortner, men, lacking the natural procreative abilities of women, exhibit their creativity externally through the manipulation of symbols in such activities as art and through involvement in public affairs beyond the family. Their activities thus "make culture" and are regarded as quintessentially cultural by members of the group, just as mating and marriage outside the family group in Lévi-Strauss' scheme are associated with the cultural. Thus, men transcend nature while women lack this ability.

Ortner draws her conclusion that men are seen as superior to women because their creative abilities are not tied to the natural body from Beauvoir. This view is evident from the following statement from *The Second Sex* that Ortner quotes in her article:

> Here we have the key to the whole mystery. On the biological level the species is maintained only by creating itself anew; but this creation results only in repeating the same Life in more individuals. But man assures the repetition of life while transcending Life through Existence [i.e. goal-oriented, meaningful action]; by this transcendence he creates values that deprive pure repetition of all value. In the animal, the freedom and variety of male activities are vain because no project is involved. Except for his services to the species, what he does is immaterial. Whereas in serving the species, the human male also remodels the face of the earth, he creates new instruments, he invents, he shapes the future. (Beauvoir quoted in Ortner 1974:75)

According to Ortner, because human society arose when humans made the transition from nature to culture, natural processes are devalued in relationship to cultural ones in all societies. Women's social roles, associated as they are with nature, are considered to be of a lower order than those of men. This circumstance is not one that just occurs in some societies. Indeed, Ortner asserts her arguments are "intended to apply to generalized humanity; they grow out of the human condition, as humanity has experienced and confronted it up to the present day" (1974:74).

Women as Mediators of Nature and Culture

Ortner asserts that a complicating factor arises in classifying women as natural because, at some level, it must also be recognzied that women are cultural beings. They are not, after all, living in the same state of nature as other animals. Another complication arises when women's role as the socializer of children is considered. This role involves the conversion of animal-like infants into socialized or cultural beings (Ortner 1974:84). Because of this activity, women actually mediate between nature and culture. Ortner argues that this intermediate position accounts for the ambiguous way in which women are represented in cultural ideology. On the one hand, for example, they are often symbolized negatively in myth, religion, and art as witches or castrating mothers. On the other hand, they can be depicted positively as transcendent figures, such as in the United States when a statue of a blindfolded woman is used to represent the ideal of justice as fair.

While women are subordinate to men in all societies, according to Ortner, this status is due not to some natural debility or limitation but to women everywhere being *thought* of as natural. Since the realm of nature is conceptualized as inferior to the realm of culture, which is the domain of men, women are thought of as inferior to men.

The Self/Other Dichotomy

The nature/nurture dichotomy is tied, according to Ortner, to another set of categories: that of the Self and Other, in which men are associated with the first term and women with the second. According to Beauvoir, a man knows what he is by knowing what he is not. And man is not woman. Thus for men, selfhood is created through a comparison with individuals who occupy the category Other, that is, women. And women are Other because they are defined by their bodies while men are defined by a self that floats free of bodily functions. Beauvoir argued that men profit from the Otherness of women. Men have created this concept of woman's nature as Other, as trapped in the body, while they have imagined themselves as transcendent, associated with mind, which is an entity free from the constraints of the body (Conboy, Medina, and Stanbury 1997:2). As Conboy and her associates put it, this entrapment of women in their bodies means that "women have been made the other and the other is inferior—'the second sex,' always defined by a lack of masculine qualities that men assume results from natural defectiveness" (1997:7).

Beauvoir demonstrated that the Self/Other, subject/object, man/woman, masculine/feminine, mind/body divisions so pervasive in Western thought are part of a system of oppositions that deprives women of autonomous selfhood and defines men as the central actors in culture. Since woman has been defined by her body, and this definition has rendered her as object not as subject, as passive not as active, feminists have searched to uncover the ways in which women continue to internalize the values associated with being a body/object. As we will see in the next chapter, recent studies have focused on how women are continuously reminded of the central role their bodies play in their self-perception.

CRITIQUE OF ORTNER

While Ortner's work has been important in furthering thinking about how cultural categorizations and ideas affect women, it can also be questioned. For example, not all anthropologists accept her assertion that women in all societies are devalued. She based this conclusion on the information received by anthropologists from informants during fieldwork. But as Karen Sacks has suggested, there were few anthropologists prior to the 1970s who actually asked members of other societies "who is worth more, men or women?" Instead, anthropologists tended to translate symbolic statements and forms of behavior into answers to this question, offering interpretations that may have been based on their own Western assumptions. It has also been argued that it is men's valuation of women that is given preeminence in Ortner's formulation, not the value women place on themselves. For example, Carol MacCormack (1980) reports conversations with women informants who are chiefs and heads of descent groups, secret societies, and households. MacCormack points out that they would not agree with the statement that women are inferior to men (p. 16).

Ortner can also be criticized for invoking evidence of female subordination selectively. While she uses instances in which women are viewed as defiling as an indicator of female devaluation and subordination, she does not interpret the symbol of justice in the United States, for example, as indicating a high status for women. Instead this construction is explained by the proposed intermediate position of women between nature and culture and is interpreted as a symbolic resolution of this ambiguous position.

ORTNER'S LATER WORK

Ortner has responded to these criticisms and has refined and expanded her ideas about gender in important ways since writing "Is Female to Male as Nature Is to Culture?" For instance, she has pointed out that gender is always at least in part situated on the nature/culture border of the body, which is always gendered. Thus, she claims, gender becomes a powerful language for talking about important philosophical questions of nature and culture in many cultures (Ortner 1996:180).

She also suggests in her recent book, *Making Gender: The Politics and Erotics of Culture*, that while the idea that nature must be overcome by culture may be a Western construction, all humans must cope with the limits nature places on them (1996:179). This position is consistent with her "practice" approach to anthropology. As we have seen, this form of analysis is interested in how society as a system constrains people's actions while, at the same time, society is made through human action and interaction (Ortner 1984:159).

Anthropologists using this approach have tended to focus on traditional societies and have viewed them largely as isolated, unaffected by outside forces. In her most recent work, Ortner (1996) has shown the need to expand traditional anthropological notions of "the system" to include the impact of Western ideas and institutions on non-Western women's options. For example, she argues that among the Sherpa of the Himalayas today, Sherpa women have to negotiate a complex context of gender meanings. This context includes not only the traditional ideas and beliefs of their culture but also media representations and international mountain climbing expeditions where Sherpa men act as guides for Western participants who put their own ideas about male and female roles into play.

CONCLUSIONS

Regardless of the specific drawbacks of a structuralist interpretation of gender roles and sexual asymmetry, its insights have been valuable. So have criticisms of it. As Carol Brettell and Carolyn Sargent point out, "the critique of the concepts of universal subordination and the nature-culture dichotomy" resulting from the work of such theorists as Lévi-Strauss and Ortner "has stimulated significant research on how gender identity and gender roles are constructed in particular cultural contexts" (1997:125).

In particular, the ideas of Beauvoir continue to have an important impact on anthropology and how contemporary anthropologists think and go about their own work. Beauvoir's notion of the Other as a category devised by men to construct themselves as agents capable of acting in the world has been expanded to include non-Western people. Anthropologists now scrutinize how Western researchers and writers have constructed non-Western societies as objects in need of study and analysis. This construction of the Other, they argue, acts as a backdrop against which the West can define itself and legitimize its activities. The West comes to know what it is by knowing what it is not, and it is not the Other. In this construction, some of the characteristics of the Other are: primitive, exotic, and underdeveloped. Such insights have been crucial to the reflexive orientation we discuss in chapter 8.

As culture bearers of a particular segment of your society, do your experiences support the view that women are subordinate to men, that women's bodies make them closer to nature, or that men are social actors while women are passive objects? If you take the position that women are subordinate to men, you would need to consider more than the variable of gender in order to support this contention. For example, as materialist theorists have shown, class position also has an important influence on an individual's experiences and identity. Such variables as race, religion, ethnicity, sexual orientation, and physical ability have too. As we will see in the next chapter, when a variety of social, political, economic, and religious practices and institutions are examined, it becomes clear that an individual's life chances and sense of self are enhanced and complicated by multiple layers of meaning.

Chapter Seven

Discourse Analysis and Sociolinguistic Orientations

Structuralists are not the only theorists who have been concerned with the relationship of language to gender. In anthropology, post-structural and sociolinguistic approaches also take as a primary focus the role language plays in the construction of gender identities or gender dynamics. As we will see, these two approaches differ in important ways. However, they share a focus on language as both constitutive and reflective of one's social identity and social position. They recognize that language is a productive system that is tied to how power is distributed both socially and materially in any given society.

Post-structuralists draw heavily on work done by earlier structuralists but differ from them in important ways. For example, like Lévi-Strauss, many post-structuralist thinkers are concerned with how ideas construct notions of gender and the body, but they do not appeal to underlying structures in the brain or agree that all human thinking is binary. Instead, post-structuralists see binary categories like male/female, Self/Other, and mind/body as divisions that underscore *Western* thinking, ones that have been used to rationalize existing power relations. Post-structuralist thinkers wish to break down such binary categories and go beyond them. They also call into question many of the ideas that have been central to Western ways of thinking.

Post-structuralism is quite diverse and includes the ideas of such thinkers as the philosopher Jacques Derrida; psychoanalyst Jacques Lacan; and philosopher-historian Michel Foucault, who has been called one of the most influential thinkers of the twentieth century (Miller 1993). While the work of all these theorists, as well as of other post-structuralists, has been extremely influential over the last few decades, it is Foucault's ideas that have had the greatest impact on anthropologists. Foucault's work is itself quite diverse. Thus we focus here only on his conceptualization of language as discourse and his ideas concerning the relationship of discourse to power, because these emphases have had a profound influence on how contemporary theorists conceptualize gender oppression (see, especially, Foucault 1980).

Sociolinguistics is a branch of anthropological linguistics focused on the way in which language is used in social interactions to mark status and role relationships (Smith and Young 1998). Sociolinguistic analyses tend to focus on how individuals actually speak or use language in social contexts. Thus, these studies are highly empirical, based on the close and careful observation of men and women in different societies or from different racial, ethnic, or class backgrounds. This approach goes beyond conceptualizing language as discourse in order to understand such phenomena as the differences in men's and women's speech patterns or miscommunication between the sexes.

Our goal in this chapter is to introduce you to the fundamental ideas of the post-structuralist thinker Michel Foucault, whose influence on anthropological studies of gender has been immense. Concentrating on his work in the first part of this chapter, we demonstrate the significance of post-structuralist ideas for current work on a wide range of issues related to social inequalities. Many anthropologists interested in language and its impact on gender asymmetry would not consider themselves post-structuralists. We review the work of some of these sociolinguists in the second part of this chapter, especially those whose work calls into question Foucault's inattention to gender differences in language. We end the chapter with an assessment of the strengths and weaknesses of some of Foucault's formulations.

FOUCAULT'S POST-STRUCTURALISM

Foucault, like Lévi-Strauss, was interested in language but not with its underlying structure. Instead, Foucault focused on language as discourse, as a productive system that creates people's very sense of who they are. *Discourses* are systems of knowledge, supported by institutions and practices that create a picture for people of what is true and what is not. For example, the discourse of the "religious right" in North America leads some people to believe that the family is the basis of all significant values in society and that anything that threatens it is wrong and dangerous. In this scheme, abortion is seen as evil and sinful and as an act that under all circumstances, even when a woman has become pregnant due to rape, must be prohibited and prevented. Proponents of this view claim that if women control their own bodies, the institution of the family may be eroded, leading to social downfall. This discourse is countered by another one that seems equally true and right to its adherents: if a democracy is to work, individuals must have a right to privacy and to control their own bodies. The fight between these two discourses is a struggle for power over who has the right to determine what can and cannot be done by certain groups of people.

This illustration of the political nature of discourses is only one example of how power exists within the way people think and talk about social issues. As we will see, Foucault outlined a number of other discourses that are of particular interest to feminists, especially those who are interested in the role language plays in the constitution of bodies and sexual identities. In general, researchers undertaking discourse analysis strive to identify influential societal discourses and to analyze the impact they have on people's lives. They then attempt to uncover the relationship of these constructed notions to the way power and privileges are distributed within a society. Foucault's identification of discourses of sexuality has been especially important to investigators interested in how variables other than gender affect a person's experience of oppression.

Power from Knowledge

Foucault termed discourses, like those of medicine and psychology, that obtain power through producing knowledge "normalizing discourses." These are ways of thinking that produce a certain kind of knowledge about what is considered normal and what is considered abnormal (Diamond and Quinby 1988). Until quite recently, medicine and psychology have acted, in Foucault's terminology, as "regimes of truth." In modern societies like our own, Foucault argued:

> "Truth" is centered on the form of scientific discourse and the institutions that produce it . . . it is the object, under diverse forms, of immense diffusion and consumption . . . it is produced and transmitted under the control . . . of a few great political and economic apparatuses (university, army, writing, media). (Foucault quoted in Diamond and Quinby 1988:x–xi)

Through such regimes, people's ideas and behaviors can be controlled. What is particularly important about discourses as regimes of truth, Foucault asserts, is that people cannot construct identities outside of them. Indeed, just the opposite occurs. People find meaning and identity in them. But discourses create categories of identity to sustain power relations and patterns of domination. If people think of themselves as they are purported by normalizing discourses, they will recognize themselves in talk about normality and abnormality. Individuals will inculcate these ideas, and these ideas will act to produce a person's very identity. Identity is thus a site of power in contemporary societies. It is a locus of domination through which people are controlled. Like feminists, Foucault is interested in identifying and dismantling such modes of domination, or regimes of power, and in uncovering the multiple ways in which they oppress individuals.

The Discourse of Homosexuality

The burgeoning gay rights movement of the 1970s and 1980s increased interest in questions of sexual preference among feminist researchers, especially the role sexuality plays in society to privilege some people and disadvantage others. Paradoxically, while Foucault was quite interested in the construction of homosexuality, he was critical of one of the primary strategies of the gay liberation movement: "coming out" to acknowledge publicly that one is a homosexual (Miller 1993:255). For to do so, he claimed, one must assume that there is a fixed identity to proclaim in public. Foucault contended that such a fixed identity does not exist. To say, "I am a homosexual," Foucault argued, plays into the hands of those experts, such as physicians and psychologists who, for the most part, have viewed homosexuality as deviant, unnatural, and abnormal and created this category of sexual identity. Since the nineteenth century, medicine and psychology have sought to gain knowledge of same-sex sexual behaviors and to organize this knowledge into a discourse of homosexuality. This discourse has created the very idea of "the homosexual." Foucault claimed that before this time homosexual acts occurred, but the social identity "homosexual" did not exist. Scientific discourses have created this category of identity through organizing information about same-sex sexual relations under the heading "homosexuality." This creation of categories of identity is a problem, Foucault argued, because having knowledge of something allows power and control (domination) over it.

Counter Discourses

Foucault argues that to oppose such domination or regimes of power, "counter discourses" must be developed. These are discourses that speak on behalf of the oppressed. For example, the counter discourse of homosexuality that has arisen out of feminism and gay rights activism has begun to demand that homosexuality's legitimacy or naturalness be acknowledged. It has called for an alternative understanding of homosexuality, one that does not see it as abnormal, sick, or unnatural as traditional medical and psychological discourses have tended to do (Diamond and Quinby 1988:xi). Indeed, the recent acceptance by some gay men and lesbians of studies suggesting that homosexuality may have a genetic basis can be understood within this context. In the United States and in other Western societies, if something has a biological base, it is often deemed natural. Those who accept this conclusion hope that claiming a natural basis for homosexuality will change the view that it is abnormal and alterable. Opponents of this view, however, argue that the evidence used to substantiate a genetic basis of homosexuality is weak. They warn against ready acceptance of this view given the way biological information traditionally has been used to oppress groups of people.

Feminism is also a counter discourse. For example, it contests notions of femininity that construct the female as docile, dependent, and inferior, notions promulgated, as we have seen, in such discourses as social evolutionism, sociobiology, and classical psychoanalysis. In general, Foucault's ideas about regimes of truth and power have prompted feminists to be suspicious of all discourses that claim to know what is "true" and what is "natural." The idea inherent in Foucault's formulation—that power is embedded in our very sense of who we are—has also been important to feminists because it resonates with the feminist claim that "the personal is political." This slogan has fueled feminist studies since the 1970s. It has spurred countless feminist inquiries into how power and domination operate at the most intimate levels of women's lives.

THE FEMINIST CRITIQUE OF FOUCAULT

While feminists have found Foucault's ideas about discourse, knowledge, and power exciting and useful, they have also pointed to Foucault's lack of interest in discourses that construct masculinity and femininity and to his failure to distinguish between discourses that may construct male and female bodies and sexuality differently. Indeed, feminists have suggested that, in some ways, Foucault was like the humanists he criticized. Just as humanists have developed the idea of universal "man" by using privileged white males as the standard, Foucault developed ideas about a universal "body" that invoked the white male body as the norm (see Mascia-Lees and Sharpe 1992). This treatment of the male body as the standard form has prompted feminists to investigate the particular ways in which the female body and sexuality are a locus of power and control.

Some feminist researchers, for example, have focused on how the notions of beauty in popular discourses have led women to engage in life-threatening practices, such as self-starvation (*anorexia nervosa*) (see, for example, Bordo 1993) or breast implants (see, for example, Wolf 1992). Often women are motivated to alter their bodies by a desire to bring them into closer conformity with societal expectations and to enhance their own sense of who they are. Such discourses, some feminists argue, lie at the very base of women's sense of self and of their own self-worth.

DISCOURSES OF THE FEMALE BODY

Emily Martin's book, *The Woman in the Body* (1987), is particularly revealing of the ways North American medical discourse and research perpetuate negative images of women's bodies. Martin begins her analysis by questioning why women in North American society tend to view themselves as fragmented, as lacking a sense of autonomy, and as feeling carried along by forces beyond their control (1987:194). She suggests that these feelings may be due, in part, to the way the medical profession constructs notions of the female body. It uses metaphors of production, for example, in its description of childbirth in which women are seen as passive laborers in a process in which doctors produce a desirable "product" in the form of a healthy child.

Martin's analysis of the descriptions of women's bodily functions in medical textbooks reveals that they are far from the objective depictions one might suppose. The metaphors that have been used to explain female bodily processes like menstruation and menopause have not been drawn from science, but from aspects of Western economic systems. Menstruation, for example, has been likened to the failure of a factory system: the female body fails to create a useful embryo, instead producing a worthless product, menstrual blood. Menstruation is therefore a productive system gone awry (Martin 1987:46). Martin shows that medical texts describe menopause through a language derived from the communication industry with its focus on "information-transmitting systems with a hierarchical structure" (Martin 1987:41). Martin describes the depiction of menopause in one of these texts thus:

> In menopause, according to a college text, the ovaries become "unresponsive" to stimulation from the gonadotropins, to which they used to respond. As a result, the ovaries "regress." On the other end of the cycle, the hypothalamus has gotten estrogen "addiction" from all those years of menstruating. As a result of the withdrawal of estrogen at menopause, the hypothalamus begins to give "inappropriate orders.". . . what is being described is the breakdown of the system of authority. . . . At every point in the system, functions "fail" and falter. (1987:42)

This portrayal of menopause as a failure of the authority structure of the body contributes to our society's negative view of it. As the author of one textbook says, with the onset of menopause "a woman must readjust her life from one that has been physiologically stimulated by estrogen and progesterone production to one devoid of these hormones" (Guyton quoted in Martin 1987:51). This statement implies that women cannot continue a vigorous life after menopause (they are no longer "stimulated") and must think of themselves as lacking something that invigorated them previously (they are now "devoid" of hormones).

North American society is not the only one that has constructed negative notions of female bodily processes. For example, in many societies menstruating women are viewed as polluting and dangerous, as capable of defiling anyone or anything that comes in contact with them. In some societies, this belief has given rise to taboos that require women's seclusion during their menstrual period. Such taboos, however, may not always have negative implications. Among some Native Americans, for instance, the menstrual blood of sequestered women is seen as a source of power (Buckley 1982).

While Martin's analysis shows how supposedly objective scientific accounts of women's bodies are informed by negative cultural assumptions, it also suggests that women are not affected equally by them. She finds that white middle-class women are more likely to hold a worldview consistent with a "scientific" one and thus are more likely to accept the views of their bodies offered by contemporary medical discourse. In contrast, women from working-class backgrounds are more likely to resist such views. Martin proposes that these different responses arise because the people most oppressed by a system are more likely to be critical of it and to call for fundamental changes in it (Martin 1987:190–91).

Race, Class, Ethnicity, and the Body

Rayna Rapp's study of amniocentesis, a technique used to reveal fetal anomalies such as Down's syndrome, has produced similar results regarding a variety of responses from women. She has shown how a woman's race, class, and ethnicity can affect her decision to abort a child who, in medical discourse, is seen as "defective." White middle-class women in her sample tended to be more ambivalent about the idea of raising a disabled child than were Latina women. According to Rapp, Latina women often recall friends and family members with sickly children and see the care given to these children by their mothers as consistent with a self-sacrificing view of motherhood that is valued by them (1990:36). Martin's and Rapp's conclusions that responses to the medicalization of women's bodies vary by ethnicity and class have also been substantiated by a number of other studies (see, for example, Ginsburg and Rapp 1991).

Studies of the impact of race on notions of the body and on definitions of femininity have been particularly revealing of the fact that while the female body may be constructed, it is not constructed evenly (Conboy, Medina, and Stanbury 1997:4). In Western culture, for example, the bodies of women of color have been variously constructed as exotic or as deviant. The bodies of Asian women have often been seen as erotic and exotic in the Western discourse of "the Orient." Their smallness has been associated with timidity and subservience, traits that have made them desirable to many men in Western societies. This perception has even led to the development of mail-order businesses in which Asian women are sold to Western male consumers as brides (Villapando 1989).

In Western societies, African-American women's bodies, by contrast, have historically been associated with an animal-like sexuality. Perhaps this belief was nowhere clearer than in Victorian England where, under the guise of scientific interest, the African woman Sartje Bartman, known as "the Hottentot Venus," was displayed nude to be probed at by anatomists and stared at by a repulsed, but fascinated, public. Her distinctive bodily traits, enlarged vaginal lips and protruding buttocks, were taken as signs of a rampant and animalistic sexuality (Gilman 1985; Gould 1985). This conclusion acted to reinforce the notion at the time that African women were savages, devoid of the sexual modesty necessary for achieving "true" femininity. As we have seen, this racist view was produced through a discourse of progress that saw all Africans as closer to animals than humans and, therefore, as inferior and less evolved.

The Disabled Body

African bodies were not the only ones displayed in public in the late nineteenth century. During this time, people with mental and physical disabilities were used as circus attractions and viewed as "freaks" by a gawking audience. Like Sartje Bartman, disabled people were offered as evidence of a "primitive" stage in cultural development (Thomson 1996). For example, the boys known as "Ancient Aztecs," who had a genetic condition characterized by a small and pointed head known as microcephaly, were promoted as descendants of a "lost primitive society" (Bogdan 1996). This assertion made sense to viewers who were steeped in the cultural discourse of progress we described in chapter 3. This discourse viewed non-Western people as mentally inferior and associated this inferiority with small brain size. The use of skull measurements to "prove" that non-Western people were intellectually inferior to Western white men of the right class can be linked to the measurement of women's brains discussed in chapter 1. The connection is not surprising. On the one hand, Western women were equated with primitives and were viewed as irrational and inferior in intelligence to Western men. On the other hand, non-Western people were feminized and were viewed like Western women as in need of protection and assistance. The West, it was claimed, was obligated to civilize "primitives," a mission termed by Rudyard Kipling "The White Man's Burden." This ideology, as we have seen, was used to justify colonialism.

Studies of contemporary discourses of the body show that disabled men continue to be feminized, while disabled women are desexualized.

Such constructions place wide-ranging constraints on the way the disabled can construct notions of identity and selfhood.

The Body as Site of Resistance

Some recent analyses of women's bodies have focused on how women resist dominant cultural discourses of the female body. One increasingly popular form of resistance found among women in the United States involves tattooing and piercing. While some commentators view these body-altering practices as little more than a stylistic fad, others have argued that they may have more significant meanings for some women. For example, Fran Mascia-Lees and Pat Sharpe found that among the young white women they interviewed, body modifications were frequently described in terms of the control they give women in a society that largely defines the ideal female body through unattainable mass media images. Many young women see body piercing as a means of accepting their body as desirable, as a way to sexualize their body on their own terms, and as a method for creating their own body, using it as a kind of canvas for their art. Other young women suggest that they use the pain produced by needles piercing their flesh as a technique to control pain, something they were unable to do in earlier circumstances in which they felt victimized (Mascia-Lees and Sharpe 1994:658).

Alan Klein (1993) has shown that men, too, modify their bodies in contemporary North American culture to resist gender constructions. He suggests that through bodybuilding, diet, and drugs men build up their bodies to accentuate the anatomical differences between men and women at a time when differences between the sexes in so many other realms of life have been called into question.

The Female Body and Contestation

The female body in other recent analyses has been treated as the site where battles between competing ideologies are fought out. In particular, a number of feminist anthropologists have focused their attention on the role that constructions of the female body and motherhood play in arguments in contemporary U.S. society. Such controversies include those over abortion rights (see Ginsburg 1990), over the custody of children of lesbian couples (Lewin 1990, 1993), and over family leave legislation (Landsman 1995).

Interestingly, the female body has recently become a site of contestation within anthropology itself in debates over the political meaning of female clitoridectomy. This custom, found in a number of African and Middle Eastern societies, involves the ritual excision of a young girl's clitoris. Some feminists have vigorously opposed and condemned this "female genital mutilation," claiming that it is a brutal form of male control of female sexuality. Others have been critical of this condemnation, claiming it arises out of ethnocentric misunderstandings about the meaning of the practice to those who undergo it (see Kirby 1987).

SOCIOLINGUISTIC APPROACHES: GENDER AND LANGUAGE

Feminist linguists have also criticized Foucault for his lack of attention to gender in his analyses of language. They have argued that language is not gender-free and have also studied language's differential impact on individuals who are not white, male, and middle or upper class.

Dominant Terminology

Some feminist researchers have argued that women are subsumed by generic masculine terms in language, which renders them derivative and invisible. For example, the word "man" is used when referring to both men and women and the pronoun "he" is used when both men and women are the antecedent. Others argue that language also trivializes and degrades women through the use of such derogatory metaphors as "baby" and "chick" (Diamond and Quinby 1988:xv). Studies show that women are not only often invisible in language but are also frequently defined in terms of their sexuality, and not in flattering terms. Julia Stanley's research reports that there are more than 200 terms for sexually active women compared to approximately 20 such terms for men (Stanley cited in Nielsen 1990:20). Anthropologist Shirley Ardener (1975) has described how language can suppress women in other ways. She claims that women are a "muted" group whose voices are often silenced because their experiences are not easily expressed through the dominant communication system of their culture, one that has been developed to serve male interests.

Cross-Gender Communication

Other researchers have focused on how language operates to disadvantage women in conversations between men and women. In an early study of this type, Dale Spender (1980) noted that there is a long history in Western culture of women being stereotyped as the talkative sex, even though studies document the tendency of men to talk more than women in conversations between men and women. She suggests that this discrepancy exists because women are not being compared to men, but are being compared to silence, so that any talk by women is seen as too much. Other studies have shown that English-speaking men control conversations with women by talking more and by interrupting them frequently.

How misunderstandings arise in discussions between men and women has also been a focus of feminist analyses of gender and language. These studies suggest that cross-gender communication is prone to misinterpretation because of the differences in men's and women's communication styles. According to anthropologist Deborah Tannen:

> Women and men have different past experiences. . . . Boys and girls grow up in different worlds. . . . And as adults they travel in different worlds, reinforcing patterns established in childhood. These cultural differences include different expectations about the role of talk in relationships and how it fulfills that role. (1987:125)

Other theorists have stressed that language is interactive and have called for studies of miscommunication to focus on language as an active process whose primary goal may not be to engage in polite conversation. As Henley and Kramarae argue:

> Discussions of miscommunication seldom . . . talk about *anger* and *frustration* as emotions and expressions present *during* the conversation, not only as a result of miscommunication. Women's anger in particular has frequently been denied or interpreted in terms of misunderstanding, inarticulation, and confusion. (1994:397, emphases in the original)

Language and Race

The dominant form of communication in the United States is also problematic in terms of racist assumptions. Robert Moore (1988) shows, for example, that Standard American English is permeated with racist stereotypes at multiple levels. This language includes not only obvious words of bigotry but also meanings that encode things white as good and pure and things black as evil and sinister. Moore asks us to think about the following phrases and their connotations: you blacken one's name, blackball an enemy, and blacklist an undesirable person. But frivolous lies are white, and the good guys in the old cowboy movies wore white hats and rode white horses.

Moore extends his analysis of terms that encode judgments to include those that label certain experiences as derivative. The phrases used in chapter 5 by dependency theorists are an example: underdeveloped countries are judged in relationship to developed ones and Third World nations take last place when compared to First World and Second World nations. Both of these phrases use the dominant white cultures of the West as the norm and standard for judging what is best.

Henley and Kramarae (1994) also take race into account in their analysis of language. They call particular attention to how "problematic talk," such as cross-gender communication, is different for white women than for women of color. Women of color from matrifocal households like those described in chapter 5, for example, may not experience the same difficulties in conversations with men as white women because they have not grown up in patriarchal families. They may, however, experience quite a bit of difficulty in communication with white women.

CONCLUSIONS

While we have provided critiques of Foucault's work, we do not mean to downplay the importance of many of his insights. His ideas continue to influence researchers concerned with the way discourses construct and perpetuate power differentials and systems of oppression. In particular, his insights help explain how many Western societies continue to dictate to women a sense of self-worth that is intimately related to their physical bodies. One only has to recognize the enormous amount of money spent every year by women in Western societies on products that they hope will enhance them physically to see that this is so. From eye shadow to foot cream, women buy "beauty" in a bottle.

Theorists following Foucault have also shown how knowledge of the Other has allowed the dominant societies of the West to control non-Western societies. As we discussed in chapter 3, organizing knowledge of the non-West was a primary concern of early anthropologists whose work was influenced by colonialism. Anthropology, therefore, can itself be understood as a regime of power, one that tells the "truth" about other societies. Foucault's identification of anthropology as a discourse of power has led many anthropologists to think critically about what they do. It has raised questions about how anthropologists organize knowledge about non-Western societies. The approach that has as its starting point this kind of self-critique is called the "reflexive orientation." It shares with other post-structuralist approaches a suspicion of Western categories, a focus on language and the politics of representation, and an understanding of the constructed nature of "difference," whether gender, sexual, racial, ethnic, or cultural.

As we will see in the next chapter, the reflexive orientation also differs somewhat from the other approaches to gender that we have surveyed. For example, it is often not as interested in explaining women's oppression as it is in understanding the oppression of men and women around the world and the role anthropology has played in that oppression.

Chapter Eight

The Reflexive Approach

While many feminist anthropologists adopt a reflexive stance in their inquiries, not all reflexive anthropologists see themselves as feminist. Nonetheless, the reflexive approach is inherently feminist. It has taken many insights first developed by feminists and applied them broadly. For example, just as feminists in the 1970 came to see "truths" about femininity and womanhood as constructions that supported male supremacy, so reflexive anthropologists have come to see traditional anthropological depictions of other cultures as representations that have helped support relations of domination and oppression between the West and non-West. As constructions, such conceptualizations are open to question. This awareness has led reflexive anthropologists to view societies in new ways. No longer seen as a stable and homogenized entity, culture is now understood as a system of contested meanings. Reflexive anthropologists also draw on the feminist insight that language and politics are inseparable. As we will see, they have focused on how writing techniques have perpetuated images of the non-Western as the Other and on how constructing the Other always entails relations of domination (Mascia-Lees, Sharpe, and Cohen 1989).

In this chapter we introduce the reflexive approach to research, an approach that has been adopted by some feminist anthropologists. We place this theoretical orientation within the historical context out of which it emerged, explore the self-critique anthropology has recently undergone, and assess the challenges anthropologists continue to encounter in a world of changing power relations. Such challenges have led to a reevaluation of anthropology's tradition of fieldwork and of writing descriptions of the people it studies, challenges we describe and explain throughout this chapter.

THE ROOTS OF THE REFLEXIVE APPROACH

The period of the 1960s and 1970s was one of great social and cultural upheaval throughout the world. Countries that were colonies of European nations fought wars for independence, while, at the same time, oppressed groups within Western societies began to wage their own struggles for liberation. These efforts were often linked. Many African Americans, for example, began to associate their own oppression with that of black Africans fighting colonial domination in other parts of the world and fueled the U.S. civil rights movement.

People in the United States who demonstrated against the Vietnam War also connected their protests to colonial struggles. They saw their contestation as one against colonial rule in Vietnam, first by the French and then by the United States which continued French efforts to squash a movement for self-rule. The United States government framed the war as one against communism, promoting it as necessary for protecting free-market capitalism and democracy. But this rationale was questioned seriously by many young people who also began to critique what capitalism had wrought on its own turf: poverty and deep-seated inequality.

As we saw in the first chapter, political protests over inequality during this period were important influences on the rise of second wave feminism in the United States. By the 1970s, white women, African-American men and women, and members of other ethnic minorities, such as Native Americans, waged battles against their own oppression, just as many colonized people around the world had done. The roots of the reflexive approach in anthropology began to grow within this cultural milieu.

The Colonial Critique

Independence movements broke down traditional power relations. As a consequence, the standard ways of seeing the world and the place of different kinds of societies within it were questioned by newly liberated people, and they were found faulty. Traditional explanations of social relations were especially criticized for the role they played in developing biased images of colonized people and, thus, for how they helped maintain unequal relations between the colonized and their colonizers. In the United States, Native American groups, for example, protested images of themselves that had been created in anthropology and some called for closing the doors to anthropological research altogether (see Deloria 1988).

This scrutiny developed into full-fledged efforts to question the representations of non-Western societies in the work of Western writers.

For example, Edward Said (1979) a literary critic of Middle Eastern descent, questioned how Western writers had constructed a discourse of "the Orient," one that produced images of Eastern societies as exotic. According to Said, "the Orient" has never actually existed. It is a fabrication based on Western fantasies, one that turns Eastern societies into objects for consumption by Western spectators. Said's work has been the impetus for a wide range of critiques of similarly exoticizing and objectifying representations in a number of academic disciplines, including anthropology.

Anthropology and Self-Critique

In the wake of such criticisms, many anthropologists themselves began to recognize the limitations of traditional anthropological practices in their own research. They questioned not only previous representations of non-Western people, but also traditional explanatory models, finding many insufficient for understanding a fundamentally changed world. Anthropology by this time had moved well beyond its roots in social evolutionism. Nonetheless, critics argued that it still perpetuated inequalities between the West and what has come to be known as the "Rest" (the traditional societies that anthropologists have studied). Theoretical orientations such as structuralism, for example, were criticized for assuming that Western categories like subject/object and nature/culture were universals, rather than recognizing them as Western categories that helped to keep people "in their place."

These kinds of criticisms gave rise to a new *reflexive anthropology*, one greatly influenced by feminist anthropologists. Reflexive anthropologists think critically about the political and ethical questions surrounding their work. These anthropologists have focused specifically on how unequal power relations are reproduced in anthropological fieldwork and in ethnographic representations.

CAN THERE BE A FEMINIST ETHNOGRAPHY?

In the past, fieldwork has been the hallmark of anthropological training, and this experience has been one of the characteristics that differentiated the discipline from other social science fields, especially sociology. The expectation was that novice anthropologists would become participant-observers, usually for the period of one year, in the society they were studying. Reflexive anthropologists have questioned the context of most traditional fieldwork, raising questions about the inequality inherent to most fieldwork situations: anthropologists are primarily privileged individuals from Western societies while those they study are often oppressed people from non-Western societies. Feminists have voiced this concern most strongly, questioning how an equal relationship can exist between researcher and research subject under these conditions.

Several feminists have framed this issue by asking whether there can be a truly "feminist ethnography," one that is consistent with the feminist commitment to equality (Abu-Lughod 1990/91; Stacey 1988). Judith Stacey argues that feminist ethnographers may come close to producing fully feminist ethnographies but will never be able to completely do so. She asserts that no matter how much collaboration there is between ethnographers and the people they study, it is the ethnographers who ultimately control the final ethnographic account, granting anthropologists a power their research subjects do not have.

Other feminists have argued that truly feminist research may be possible. They suggest that the moment feminist researchers begin to address the experiences of women and other oppressed people in their work, their investigations will necessarily become concerned with questions of power and political struggle, and their research goals will be defined by that struggle. Sandra Harding argues that this focus on the political is almost inevitable because

> the questions an oppressed group wants answered are rarely requests for so-called pure truth. Instead, they are questions about how to change its conditions; how its world is shaped by forces beyond it, how to win over, defeat or neutralize those forces arrayed against its emancipation, growth or development. (1987:8)

According to this viewpoint, anthropologists can produce feminist ethnographies if they design their research questions according to what members of the oppressed groups they study want and need (see Mascia-Lees, Sharpe, and Cohen 1989). This task is not unproblematic, however, since there are often conflicting desires among people within societies. Nancy Scheper-Hughes (1995) has suggested that all ethnographers move in the direction of a "militant" anthropology that is morally engaged and openly committed to aiding the people being studied in their political struggle against oppression.

Many feminist ethnographers, white and privileged, have been encouraged to scrutinize their research efforts because of criticisms raised by some "Third World" women and women of color (see Trinh 1989). These critics have tended to agree with Stacey's position rather than with Harding's, arguing against the possibility of equality in ethnographic investigations. Many critics have viewed white feminist efforts to study and write about non-Western people as exploitative. Western writers, they claim, "speak for" the oppressed instead of allowing the oppressed to "speak for themselves."

White feminists who have replied to this criticism argue that their work actually gives voice to many people around the world who are otherwise silenced by oppression. The post-colonial writer Gayatri Spivak argues that for the Western writer, choosing "not to speak" may be just another alibi for ignoring the Other. She encourages Western researchers to "learn how to occupy the . . . position of the other rather than simply say, 'O.K., sorry, we are just very good white people, therefore we do not speak for the blacks.'" She argues that this stance acts as just another "kind of breast-beating that is left behind at the threshold" so that "business goes on as usual" (Spivak 1990:121).

Whether ethnographers silence or enable the non-Western people they write about is part of a vexed and complicated debate that has no single "right" answer. The complexity of this situation does suggest, however, that researchers committed to feminist goals must be ever-vigilant in their self-reflection about their own motivations for undertaking research and their research goals.

THE PROBLEM OF OBJECTIVITY

Not only has traditional fieldwork in most cases taken place between people of unequal status because of national origin or race, it has also put anthropologists in a superior position, that of informed scientific researcher. As knowledgeable experts, ethnographers have been expected to produce objective accounts of other people's lives that are not merely reflections of how these people see themselves. While this expectation of objectivity might seem reasonable, it is actually quite problematic.

In Western societies, objectivity is associated with science, which is understood as a higher way of knowing, one that produces the "truth" about what something is and how it operates. It is, in Foucaultian terms, a normalizing discourse. If anthropological representations are objective and scientific, people have often concluded that they must be truthful accounts of other societies. But this conclusion is based on the assumption that a human researcher, like a scientific instrument, can collect data unsullied by subjective concerns. This task, of course, is impossible. No human being can stand completely outside of the cultural context that has given rise to his or her very identity and sense of personhood. Anthropologists' perceptions and conclusions are therefore necessarily filtered through their own cultural lenses.

Yet, for the most part, traditional anthropological accounts have been taken as accurate representations, and many anthropologists have seen their work as just that. Indeed, early anthropologists often claimed scientific objectivity as a means of distinguishing their efforts from other forms of cross-cultural encounters that they claimed were less accurate. For example, travel to other societies was portrayed as a personal experience, and travel writing was seen as a subjective account of that personal experience. Anthropologists were able to legitimize anthropology as an academic discipline by claiming their own practices as scientific and objective in comparison to travel and other types of cross-cultural interaction (Pratt 1986).

Other aspects of traditional anthropology have also produced a picture of anthropology as scientific and objective, aspects that have been studied by reflexive anthropologists. These aspects include investigations of how the denial of bodily processes and sensations has constructed an ethnographer as a scientific instrument, how traditional forms of writing obscure the subjective nature of anthropological accounts, and how central anthropological concepts objectify people.

The Illusion of Objectivity: Denying the Body

The appearance of impartiality in anthropological accounts traditionally has been established by suppressing the anthropologist's identity as a person who has bodily and psychological characteristics that might affect his or her ethnographic description. Thus, anthropologists have been expected to make no reference to their own desires in their ethnographic writing, to deny emotions, and to disregard the sensuous aspects of life in another society—its smells, sounds, and flavors. These aspects of the field endeavor are associated in Western culture with the body and the particular, rather than with the mind and the transcendent. The mind has been seen as transcendent precisely because it is understood as detached from a particular knower. Thus, to produce "objective" accounts, the discipline has required that an anthropologist's subjective experiences like bodily desires and emotions be suppressed, lest they sully an otherwise "neutral" investigation.

The body and its feelings historically have been associated with the feminine in Western thinking. Thus the fact that traditional anthropology deemed these as unworthy topics of research should not be surprising. Only with the advent of feminism and post-structuralism, both of which influenced the breakdown of categories like mind/body, objective/subjective, and nature/culture, have studies of emotions (Behar 1997; Rosaldo 1989), unconscious desires (Mascia-Lees and Sharpe 1994), and sensual experiences (Stoller 1997) begun to flourish within anthropology.

The Illusion of Objectivity: The Writing of Culture

Just as an ethnographer's identity has been suppressed in fieldwork, so has it been obscured in traditional ethnographies. This denial of the anthropologist's identity has reinforced the view that ethnographies are unfiltered, scientific accounts rather than interpretations written by particular people. Establishing this veneer of objectivity has been accomplished through writing techniques, or what anthropologist Renato Rosaldo (1989) has called "classic norms of description." These norms include the rejection of using the first person personal pronoun "I" in anthropological writing and the expectation that an anthropological account will speak in generalities. In the former case, the first person is avoided to distance writers from the content of their texts. In the latter instance, descriptions of the behavior or thoughts of particular people in other societies are written about as though they describe the behavior of a whole people, "the Mbuti" or "the Ashanti," for example. This technique distances the reader from the actual people with whom anthropologists interact in the field.

Several correctives have been offered to make it clear that ethnographies are subjective accounts of individual anthropologists. These suggestions include "putting the anthropologist in the picture," whether through using first person narratives or through inserting in the text descriptions of the anthropologist, his or her assumptions, background, and personal story. These mechanisms are said to "situate" researchers. Their use allows readers of ethnographies to make their own assessments of the accuracy of an ethnographic account. Using dialogue as a form of writing has also been offered as a solution to old problems. These corrective methods show that anthropological conclusions are really the result of interactions between individuals, not the product of distanced observations of a generalized Other.

Such insights and methods had been proposed and used by many feminist anthropologists long before reflexive anthropology came to the fore in the 1980s. This is so despite the assertion made by some male proponents of reflexivity that they were creating something totally new in anthropology by calling for self-scrutiny. As Mascia-Lees, Sharpe, and Cohen put it in their critique of this assertion of inventiveness: "like European explorers 'discovering' the New World," these male champions of reflexive anthropology "perceive a new and uninhabited space where, in fact, feminists have long been at work" (1989:257). Many of the correctives proposed by reflexive anthropologists to disrupt standard anthropological assumptions are ones feminist anthropologists had adopted years before out of their concern for power inequalities. This is only one example of how feminist anthropologists' ethical and political commitments can shape theoretical and methodological concerns, thus uniting theory and practice.

A number of anthropologists, however, have been critical of the tendency in the reflexive approach to concentrate on producing "better" representations of non-Western people. This "writing culture" approach, critics argue, shifts attention away from the people anthropologists study to the texts, or ethnographies, anthropologists write. Elizabeth Enslin (1994) warns that if feminists focus too much attention on ethnographies, they will have little hope of transforming the politics of research (p. 545). She argues, quoting Claudia Salazar, that "by focusing our politics on textual innovation or critiques of them, we elude the more critical task of 'democratizing the social relations of research'" (p. 545). While not denying the influence that writing about non-Western people might have on changing perceptions of their political struggles, Enslin also urges feminist anthropologists to remain committed to such forms of political practice as teaching, activist research, and solidarity work (p. 559).

The Illusion of Objectivity: The Problem with "Culture"

Feminist and other reflexive anthropologists have been particularly successful in revealing how anthropology's traditional concepts create an illusion of objectivity. This success arises because, as Lila Abu-Lughod (1990) argues, women and "halfie" anthropologists, people with a mixed national or cultural identity, have themselves been constructed as the Other. They are in a position that allows them to be especially sensitive to the problems with traditional ways of knowing. As people who have themselves been objectified, they may be better able to recognize the limitations of a concept that objectifies other people (Mascia-Lees, Sharpe, and Cohen 1989).

Reflexive anthropologists, whether feminist, "halfie," or otherwise, have questioned some of anthropology's most fundamental concepts for just such limitations. Even "culture," the concept upon which the entire discipline has been erected, has come under attack for its "Othering" tendencies. Critics have argued that, like the concept "race," the discipline's concept categorizes people into discrete groups, when most people's social identities are more complex.

The concept of "culture" is problematic for other reasons as well. The idea that people belong to groups known as cultures, some say, traditionally has kept "difference" in place (Abu-Lughod 1990). Its use has given rise to the belief that there is something distinct that can be studied as an object. Culture, however, is not a thing that can be seen, touched, or bounded. We are led to believe that it is because we reify the concept. That is, we take this conceptual category and treat it as if it is real. We think of culture as an entity with a concrete or material existence that is "out there" and as something we can observe and objectively know if we use the right method or assumptions. Thus, reflexive anthropologists claim that the concept of culture aids in the construction of non-Western people as objects in need of distanced, scientific analysis.

ALTERNATIVE WAYS OF THINKING
ABOUT CULTURE

If culture is not real, then what should we make of all those anthropological accounts of other cultures? Why study anthropology, or any other social science for that matter, if they all reify social categories and treat them as real, actual, and true, when in actuality they are not?

To find the value in ethnographies, some feminist anthropologists have argued that they must be understood in a new way. If ethnographies are viewed as depictions of a process of interaction, rather than as descriptions of discrete and isolated entities, they take on new meaning. This reconceptualization shifts attention away from the idea that ethnography is an accurate portrait written by "us," primarily people from Western cultures, about "them," primarily people from non-Western societies. Instead it causes us to recognize ethnographies as subjective depictions of cultural interactions that involve people from two or more societies. It thereby breaks down the concepts of Self and Other. This understanding also contextualizes and embodies knowledge. It shows that ideas are a product of particular individuals who are embedded in historical and social contexts. Knowing these contexts puts us in a better position to assess for ourselves the conclusions reached by anthropologists and other writers.

Discourse vs. Culture

To overcome problems inherent to the concept of "culture," and to capture the intricacies of the contemporary world, Lila Abu-Lughod (1990) suggests that anthropologists should replace the concept of "culture" with that of "discourse." Discourse, she argues, allows for more complexity in understanding the forces acting to shape people and their experiences, because a person can be exposed to and constructed within various discourses at the same time. A black man's identity, for example, is partly constituted through a discourse of race and partly through a discourse of masculinity. While the first places him in a disadvantaged position within a system of racial hierarchy, the second may privilege him within a system of gender hierarchy. Understanding the multiple ways in which a black man, or any other person, is constructed through intersecting and even contradictory discourses produces a more complex and accurate picture than a construct like "culture" allows.

Travel vs. Culture

Other critics have suggested that, despite early anthropologists' attempts to distinguish their efforts from those of travelers, the concept of "travel" actually may be more appropriate than "culture" for understanding today's interconnected world. They argue that the metaphor of travel provides a more complex understanding of people's experiences in a world characterized by the movement of people between places and identities (Clifford 1997; Kaplan 1996). As Anna Lowenhaupt Tsing says in her ethnography *In the Realm of the Diamond Queen*, "in defining itself as a science that can travel anywhere, anthropology has classically constituted its object—'cultures'—as essentially immobile" (1993:123). In the contemporary world, however, the people of these "cultures" travel at least as much as anthropologists (Tsing 1993:124). Once the idea of static, immobile cultures is replaced with the idea of travelling people, Tsing argues, new areas of research open.

Borderlands vs. Culture

A number of anthropologists have suggested that "culture" be replaced with the concept of "borderlands," an idea that has arisen out of ethnic studies in which many researchers, like "halfie" anthropologists, write from the border between different ethnic identities (Ortner 1996). As with travel, the idea of borderlands focuses attention on intersocietal relationships and interaction, rather than on societies as static entities bounded in space (see, for example, Behar 1994; Rosaldo 1989).

Critique of Alternatives

Many anthropologists disagree with such reconceptualizations of culture. Christoph Brumann (1999), for example, argues that the concept of culture need not necessarily imply a bounded, homogeneous, coherent, stable entity. He suggests that we need not abandon the concept itself but only the uses of it that inscribe these meanings. Naomi Quinn argues that alternative concepts, such as "travel" or "borderlands," that focus on flux are antipsychological and

> fly in the face of what we know about the durability and motivational force of so many cultural understandings. In this view people are without a history of life experiences or a durable fund of self-understandings, motives, or plans for action. (personal communication 1999; see also Strauss and Quinn 1997)

We must be cautious, then, in our criticism of the idea of culture not to replace it with concepts that are equally problematic for our understanding of the complex ways in which people live and act within diverse social contexts.

Moreover, Renato Rosaldo suggests that while new concepts may be helpful in overcoming some past problems with ethnographic representation, no concept, discourse, or mode of interpretation is entirely neutral. He thus argues that we also need to develop measures for assessing ethnographic writing. One criterion might be to ask what effect ethnographic descriptions have on the reader. Do forms of description distance the reader of ethnographies so much that the people depicted in them appear unfamiliar and exotic? If the same language of description were used to represent the culture of the anthropologist or reader, would it seem valid and accurate? Another approach is to allow the people anthropologists write about to evaluate the ethnographies written about them and to take their criticisms seriously (Rosaldo 1989:50-51).

CONCLUSIONS

The reflexive approach in anthropology does not preclude other forms of feminist investigation. One can, for example, focus on the effects of material conditions or of ideas on people's lives while simultaneously keeping in mind the limitations of one's approach. This awareness encourages all researchers to question how any theoretical orientation helps frame research in ways that might not be beneficial to the people being studied, and this is no less true of the reflexive approach itself. The significance of self-reflexivity lies in the constant evaluation and reevaluation it calls for. This evaluative process better enables us all to remain aware of how power relations continue to operate, not merely in anthropological research, but more importantly in the larger world. If this process enables each of us to be more aware of, and to circumvent, power relations in our daily interactions with different people, feminist anthropology's commitment to fighting oppression becomes more realizable.

Chapter Nine

The Relevance of Anthropology to the Contemporary World

As the preceding chapters suggest, the impact of feminism on anthropology since the 1970s has been substantial. Feminist anthropology has yielded a vast body of data on the lives of women and men in our contemporary world. It has also provided invaluable insights into the causes of inequalities and the workings of systems of oppression around the world.

Nonetheless, reactions to feminist insights both inside and outside academia have been mixed. For example, the North American women's movement has undoubtedly allowed many women in the United States greater access to societal resources and privileges. Some have hailed these results as a great advance toward equality. Others have complained that they have not always benefited women equally due to other forms of stratification such as race and class, a critique that has led many feminists to a broader understanding of the workings of oppression. Still others have bemoaned the impact that changes in women's position have had on "traditional" values and ways of life in Western countries, such as the United States and Canada.

Unfortunately, people holding this latter position have often resorted to negative characterizations of feminists in an attempt to belittle their calls for equality. For example, in the last few decades the media have repeatedly portrayed feminists as male-bashing, men-hating fanatics. This representation, however, is a caricature, one that represents feminist efforts as dangerous, playing on people's fears and insecurities about change.

Feminism is so broad that many people now refer to *feminisms*. Thus, to characterize feminists in any one particular way oversimplifies the diversity of ideas, strategies, and goals that can be called feminist. Moreover, depicting feminists as extremists who enforce their views through a process called "political correctness" overlooks how most feminists actually work for social change. The majority of feminists meet their ethical commitment to equality by operating within pre-existing institutions such as educational systems, government agencies, and nonprofit political organizations. In such settings they work to inform people peacefully and reasonably about continuing gender inequities, to advocate for equality, and to provide women and other disadvantaged people with opportunities to overcome their oppression.

GENDER IN THE CONTEMPORARY WORLD

Significant changes in women's opportunities have occurred over the past few decades in a number of Western societies. In some countries, these advancements have been vociferously protested. In the United States, for example, some people have argued that continued calls for women's advancement through such policies as affirmative action now tip the scales in favor of women and actually discriminate against men. Similar claims have been made against the affirmative action taken to increase the representation of people of color in employment and in colleges and universities.

Such arguments do not acknowledge the discrimination and disadvantages women and people of color continue to experience in North American society and around the world. For example, in the United States, their wages still lag behind white men's. They are often the last hired and then the first fired (*U.S. News and World Report* in Angeloni 1997/98:145). Videotaped interactions between white salespeople and black customers reveal astonishing levels of discrimination against blacks. In the workplace, the high incidence of sexual harassment suggests that many men in the United States continue to devalue women and treat them as sexual objects.

In the context of today's global world, women for the most part fare far worse than men. In 1980, the United Nations reported: "Women, half of the world's population, did two thirds of the world's work, earned one tenth of the world's income and owned one hundredth of the world's property" (quoted in Angeloni 1997:145).

According to a 1994 analysis by *U.S. News and World Report*, not much has improved in the intervening years because the economic gains of the past decade have not always benefited women. In the former

Soviet Union, women are shunted into second-rate jobs; in China, with its booming economy, most of the people working under deplorable conditions in sweatshops in order to make prosperity possible are women; in Islamic countries death threats are issued against women advocating equal rights; in India, where boys are valued more highly than girls, reproductive technologies are used to select against the birth of daughters. Moreover, the majority of the world's women are poor, and in many countries around the world, there has been a "global epidemic of violence against women" (*U.S. News and World Report* in Angeloni 1997:145).

THE CONTINUED RELEVANCE OF GENDER STUDIES

Such inequalities suggest that there is still much work to be done to uncover the sources of oppression that exist worldwide. As we have seen, the trend in anthropology is away from asking questions about women's oppression in general and is toward investigating causes of inequalities in particular cultural contexts. These investigations have until recently proceeded within the framework of particular theoretical orientations that help guide a researcher through an otherwise overwhelmingly complicated and complex set of variables and factors. The tendency in more current work, however, is toward studies that combine the strengths of particular theoretical orientations while eschewing some of their weaker points. Post-structuralist researchers, for example, may well be interested in how a particular discourse constructs certain women's identities. However, they might at the same time look for the material conditions that support and reinforce the popularity and believability of that discourse. Such a researcher might also be concerned with how investigating these questions in another culture reproduces problematic Western notions about non-Western cultures. As more and more studies of this type are undertaken in the years to come, it is our hope that we can come closer not only to isolating the determinants of women's roles and status in particular societies but also to identifying the best course of action for overcoming all forms of discrimination and oppression.

CONCLUSIONS

The world of the twenty-first century will be greatly influenced by a generation of students like you. Over the years our own students have let us know what anthropological insights have offered them. One, for example, recently wrote about how greatly anthropology's sensitivity to difference and to systems of inequality had helped him in teaching "international understanding" in Japan. Another told us about how anthropology's emphasis on reflexivity and self-critique had pushed her to new levels of self-awareness, aiding her in her work for Amnesty International. Another student has used his appreciation of the value of indigenous skills to establish a nonprofit, nongovernmental organization that economically benefits communities of the Maya of southern Mexico. This organization enables contact between local people in Chiapas and visitors from other countries and also facilitates communication between these groups. Thus, the privileged people who travel there are more aware of the conditions under which disadvantaged people must try to survive in Mexico.

Whether as a teacher of English as a second language in New York City, as an environmental worker in Morocco, or even as the husband of a person from another culture, our students have pointed to anthropology's offer of a different perspective, not only about other cultures, but also, and perhaps more important, about their own. An anthropological perspective enables you to "connect the dots" of human behavior to form a coherent picture of the fast-changing contemporary world in which we live.

Our students have made it clear that feminist anthropology's commitment to challenging and rechallenging assumptions about people's "proper" place in the world has helped them to negotiate today's world with its complex intergender, interracial, intercultural, and international conflicts in an ethically and politically sensitive way. Our hope is that some of the insights in this book might also help you to do so.

References

Abu-Lughod, Lila. 1990. "Writing Against Culture." In Recapturing Anthropology: Working in the Present, edited by Richard Fox, pp. 137–62. Sante Fe: School of American Research.

_____. 1990/91. "Can there be a Feminist Ethnography?" *Women's Performance* 5:7–27.

Angeloni, Elvio. 1997/98. "The War Against Women." In *Anthropology: Annual Editions*, edited by Elvio Angeloni, pp. 145–47. Guilford, CT: Dushkin/McGraw Hill.

Ardener, Shirley, ed. 1975. *Perceiving Women*. London: Malaby.

Babcock, Barbara. 1995. "'Not in the Absolute Singular': Rereading Ruth Benedict." In *Women Writing Culture*, edited by Ruth Behar and Deborah Gordon, pp. 104–130. Berkeley: University of California Press.

Bachofen, J. J. [1861] 1992. *Myth, Religion, and Mother Right: Selected Writings of J. J. Bachofen*, translated by Ralph Manhein. Princeton, NJ: Princeton University Press.

Bamberger, Joan. 1974. "The Myth of Matriarchy: Why Men Rule in Primitive Society." In *Woman, Culture, & Society*, edited by Michelle Zimbalist Rosaldo and Louise Lamphere, pp. 263–80. Stanford, CA: Stanford University Press.

Barry, H., M. Bacon, and I. Child. 1957. "A Cross-cultural Survey of Some Sex Differences in Socialization." *Journal of Abnormal and Social Psychology* 55:327–32.

Beauvoir, Simone de. 1953. *The Second Sex*, edited and translated by H. M. Parshley. New York: Knopf.

Behar, Ruth. 1994. *Translated Woman: Crossing the Border with Esperanza's Story*. Boston: Beacon Press.

_____. 1997. *The Vulnerable Observer: Anthropology that Breaks Your Heart*. Boston: Beacon Press.

Bell, Diane. 1983. *Daughters of the Dreaming*. Melbourne: McPhee Gribble.

Bledsoe, Caroline. 1980. *Women and Marriage in Kpelle Society*. Stanford, CA: Stanford University Press.

Bogdan, Robert. 1996. "The Social Construction of Freaks." In *Freakery: Cultural Spectacles of the Extraordinary Body*, edited by Rosemarie Garland

Thomson, pp. 23–37. New York: NYU Press.

Bohannan, Paul. 1992. *We, the Alien: An Introduction to Cultural Anthropology.* Prospect Heights, IL: Waveland Press.

Bordo, Susan. 1993. *Unbearable Weight.* Berkeley: University of California Press.

Boserup, Ester. 1970. *Women's Role in Economic Development.* London: Allen and Unwin.

Bossen, Laurel Herbenar. 1984. *The Redivision of Labor: Women and Economic Choice in Four Guatemalan Communities.* New York: SUNY Press.

Brettell, Caroline and Carolyn Sargent, eds. 1993. *Gender in Cross-Cultural Perspective,* (1st ed.). Englewood Cliffs, NJ: Prentice Hall.

_____. 1997. *Gender in Cross-Cultural Perspective* (2nd ed.). Englewood Cliffs, NJ: Prentice Hall.

Brown, Judith. 1970. "A Note on the Division of Labor by Sex." *American Anthropologist* 72 (5):1073–78.

Brown, Susan. 1975. "Love Unites Them and Hunger Separates Them: Poor Women in the Dominican Republic." In *Toward an Anthropology of Women,* edited by Rayna R. Reiter, pp. 322–32. New York: Monthly Review.

Brumann, Christoph. 1999. "Writing for Culture: Why a Successful Concept Should Not Be Discarded." *Current Anthropology* 40, supplement (February): 1–13.

Buckley, Thomas. 1982. "Menstruation and the Power of Yurok Women: Methods in Cultural Reconstruction." *American Ethnologist* 9:47–60.

Burton, F. 1972. "Sexual Climax in Female *Macca mulatta.*" *Proceedings of the Third World International Congress of Primatology* 3:180–91.

Callender, Charles, and Lee Kochems. 1983. "The North American Berdache." *Current Anthropology* 24:443–70.

Caplan, Patricia. 1985. *Class and Gender in India: Women and their Organisations in a South Indian Village.* London: Tavistock.

Chodorow, Nancy. 1974. "Family Structure and Feminine Personality." In *Woman, Culture, & Society,* edited by Michelle Zimbalist Rosaldo and Louise Lamphere, pp. 43–66. Stanford, CA: Stanford University Press.

Chronicle of Higher Education, September 18, 1998, XLV (4):A18.

Clifford, James. 1997. *Routes: Travel and Translation in the Late Twentieth Century.* Cambridge: Harvard University Press.

Cohen, Colleen, and Frances E. Mascia-Lees. 1989. "Lasers in the Jungle: Reconfiguring Questions of Human and Non-Human Primate Sexuality." *Medical Anthropology,* 11(4):351–66.

Cole, Sally. 1995. "Ruth Landes and the Early Ethnography of Race and Gender." In *Women Writing Culture,* edited by Ruth Behar and Deborah Gordon, pp. 166–85. Berkeley: University of California Press.

Collier, Jane. 1974. "Women in Politics." In *Woman, Culture, & Society,* edited by Michelle Zimbalist Rosaldo and Louise Lamphere, pp. 89–96. Stanford, CA: Stanford University Press.

Conboy, K., N. Medina, and S. Stanbury. 1997. "Introduction." In *Writing on the Body: Female Embodiment and Feminist Theory,* edited by K. Conboy, N. Medina, and S. Stanbury, pp. 1–12. New York: Columbia University Press.

Conkey, Margaret. 1997. "Men and Women in Prehistory: An Archaeological Challenge." In *Gender in Cross-Cultural Perspective* (2nd ed.), edited by Caroline Brettell and Carolyn Sargent, pp. 57–66. Englewood Cliffs, NJ:

Prentice Hall.

Dahl, Gudrum. 1987. "Women in Pastoral Production: Some Theoretical Notes on Roles and Resources." *Ethnos* 52(1–2):246–79.

Dawkins, Richard. 1976. *The Selfish Gene*. New York: Oxford University Press.

de Lauretis, Teresa. 1990. "Upping the Anti[sic] in Feminist Theory." In *Conflicts in Feminism*, edited by Marianne Hirsch and Evelyn Fox Keller, pp. 255–70. New York: Routledge.

Deloria, Vine Jr. 1988. *Custer Died for Your Sins*. Norman: University of Oklahoma Press.

Diamond, Irene, and Lee Quinby. 1988. "Introduction." In *Feminism and Foucault: Reflections on Resistance*, edited by Irene Diamond and Lee Quinby, pp. ix–xx. Boston: Northeastern University Press.

di Leonardo, Micaela. 1991. *Gender at the Crossroads of Knowledge: Feminist Anthropology in the Postmodern Era*. Berkeley: University of California Press.

_____. 1997. "The Female World of Cards and Holidays: Women, Families, and the Work of Kinship." In *Gender in Cross-Cultural Perspective* (2nd ed.), edited by Caroline Brettell and Carolyn Sargent, pp. 340–50. Englewood Cliffs, NJ: Prentice Hall.

Duffy, Kevin. 1996. *Children of the Forest*. Prospect Heights, IL: Waveland Press.

Ember, Melvin, and Carol Ember. 1998. "Facts of Violence." *Anthropology Newsletter* (October):14.

Engels, Friedrich. 1884. *The Origin of the Family, Private Property and the State* (1884). Excerpted in *The Marx-Engels Reader* (2nd ed.), edited by Robert C. Tucker, pp. 734–58. New York: W.W. Norton, 1978.

Enslin, Elizabeth. 1994. "Beyond Writing: Feminist Practice and the Limitations of Ethnography." *Cultural Anthropology* 9 (4):537–68.

Evans-Pritchard, E. E. 1965. *The Position of Women in Primitive Societies and Other Essays*. New York: The Free Press.

Fedigan, Linda. 1982. *Primate Paradigms: Sex Roles and Social Bonds*. Montreal: Eden Press.

Ferree, Myra Marx, Judith Lorber, and Beth B. Hess, eds. 1999. *Revisioning Gender*. Thousand Oaks: Sage.

Finn, Janet. 1995. "Ella Cara Deloria and Mourning Dove: Writing For Cultures, Writing Against the Grain." In *Women Writing Culture*, edited by Ruth Behar and Deborah Gordon, pp. 131–47. Berkeley: University of California Press.

Foucault, Michel. 1980. *The History of Sexuality, Volume 1: An Introduction*, translated by Robert Hurley. New York: Vintage.

Frank, Gelya. 1995. "The Ethnographic Films of Barbara Myerhoff: Anthropology, Feminism, and the Politics of Jewish Identity." In *Women Writing Culture*, edited by Ruth Behar and Deborah Gordon, pp. 207–32. Berkeley: University of California Press.

Freidan, Betty. 1963. *The Feminine Mystique*. New York: Dell.

Freidel, David and Linda Schele. 1997. "Maya Royal Women: A Lesson in Precolumbian History." In *Gender in Cross-Cultural Perspective* (2nd ed.), edited by Caroline Brettell and Carolyn Sargent, pp. 74–78. Englewood Cliffs, NJ: Prentice Hall.

Freize, I., J. Parsons, P. Johnson, D. Ruble, and G. Zellman. 1978. *Women and Sex*

Roles: A Social Psychological Perspective. New York: Norton.

Freud, Sigmund. [1933] 1965. *New Introductory Lectures in Psychoanalysis*, edited and translated by J. Strachey. New York: Norton.

Gailey, Christine W. 1998. "Feminist Methods." In *Handbook of Methods in Cultural Anthropology*, edited by H. Russell Bernard, pp. 203–34. Walnut Creek, CA: Altamira.

Geertz, Clifford. 1973. *The Interpretation of Cultures*. New York: Basic Books.

Gero, Joan. 1985. "Socio-politics of Archaeology and the Woman-at-Home Ideology." *American Anthropologist* 50:342–50.

Gilligan, Carol. 1982. *In a Different Voice: Psychological Theory and Women's Development*. Cambridge: Harvard University Press.

Gilman, Sander. 1985. *Difference and Pathology: Stereotypes of Sexuality, Race, and Madness*. Ithaca, NY: Cornell University Press.

Ginsburg, Faye. 1990. "The 'Word-Made' Flesh: The Disembodiment of Gender in the Abortion Debate." In *Uncertain Terms: Negotiating Gender in American Culture*, edited by Faye Ginsburg and Anna L. Tsing, pp. 59–75. Boston: Beacon Press.

Ginsburg, Faye and Rayna Rapp, eds. 1995. *Conceiving the New World Order*. Berkeley: University of California Press.

Ginsburg, Faye and Anna L. Tsing, eds. 1990. *Uncertain Terms: Negotiating Gender in American Culture*. Boston: Beacon Press.

Goodale, Jane. [1971] 1994. *Tiwi Wives: A Study of the Women of Melville Island, North Australia*. Prospect Heights, IL: Waveland Press.

Gough, Kathleen. 1975. "The Origin of the Family." In *Toward an Anthropology of Women*, edited by Rayna R. Reiter, pp. 51–77. New York: Monthly Review.

Gould, Stephen J. 1985. *The Flamingo's Smile: Reflections in Natural History*. New York: Norton.

Gray, John. 1992. *Men are from Mars, Women are from Venus: A Practical Guide for Improving Communication and Getting What You Want in Your Relationship*. New York: HarperCollins.

Guettel, C. 1974. *Marxism and Feminism*. Toronto: Hunter Rose.

Hales, Dianne. 1998. "The Female Brain." *Ladies Home Journal* (May 1988):128, 173, 176, and 184.

Haraway, Donna. 1990. *Primate Visions: Gender, Race and Nature in the World of Modern Science*. London: Routledge.

_____. 1991. *Simians, Cyborgs, and Women: The Reinvention of Nature*. London: Routledge.

Harding, Sandra. 1987. "Introduction: Is there a Feminist Method?" In *Feminism and Methodology*, edited by Sandra Harding, pp. 1–14. Bloomington: Indiana University Press.

Harley, D. 1982. "Models of Human Evolution." *Science* 217:296.

Harrison, Faye. 1991. "Women in Jamaica's Urban Informal Economy: Insights from a Kingston Slum." In *Third World Women and the Politics of Feminism*, edited by Chandra Talpade Mohanty, Ann Russo, and Lourdes Torres, pp. 173–96. Bloomington: Indiana University Press.

Harvey, Penelope. 1998. "Feminism and Anthropology." In *Contemporary Feminist Theories*, edited by Stevi Jackson and Jackie Jones, pp. 73–85. Washington Square: New York University Press.

Henley, Nancy and Cheris Kramarae. 1994. "Gender, Power, and Miscommunication." In *The Women and Language Debate: A Sourcebook*, edited by C. Roman, S. Juhasz, and C. Miller, pp. 383–406. Piscataway, NJ: Rutgers University Press.

Herdt, Gilbert. 1982. *Rituals of Manhood: Male Initiation in Papua New Guinea*. Berkeley: University of California Press.

Hernández, Graciela. 1995. "Multiple Subjectivities and Strategic Positionality: Zora Neale Hurston's Experimental Ethnographies." In *Women Writing Culture*, edited by Ruth Behar and Deborah Gordon, pp. 148–65. Berkeley: University of California Press.

Hirsch, Marianne, and Evelyn Fox Keller. 1990. *Conflicts in Feminism*. New York: Routledge.

Hobhouse, G. C. 1924. *Morals in Evolution*. London: Chapman and Hall.

Hrdy, Sarah B. 1979. "The Evolution of Human Sexuality: The Latest Word and the Last." *Quarterly Review of Biology* 54:309–14.

_____. 1981. *The Woman That Never Evolved*. Cambridge: Harvard University Press.

Hurtado, Aida. 1989. "Relating to Privilege: Seduction and Rejection in the Subordination of White Women and Women of Color." *Signs* 14 (4):833–55.

Isaac, G. 1982. "Models of Human Evolution." *Science* 217:295.

Jacobs, Sue-Ellen, Wesley Thomas, and Sabine Lang, eds. 1997. *Two-Spirit People: Native American Gender Identity, Sexuality, and Spirituality*. Urbana: University of Illinois Press.

Johanson, Donald, and Maitland Edey. 1981a. *Lucy: The Beginnings of Humankind*. New York: Touchstone.

_____. 1981b. "How Ape Became Man: Is it a Matter of Sex?" *Science* (April):45–49.

Jones, David. 1997. *Women Warriors*. Virginia: Brassey.

Kaplan, Caren. 1996. *Questions of Travel: Postmodern Discourses of Displacement*. Durham: Duke University Press.

Kirby, Vicki. 1987. "On the Cutting Edge: Feminism and Clitoridectomy." *AFS* 5:35–55.

Klein, Alan. 1993. *Little Big Men: Bodybuilding Subculture and Gender Construction*. New York: SUNY Press.

Kratz, Corinne. 1994. *Affecting Performance: Meaning, Movement and Experience in Okiek Women's Initiations*. Washington, DC: Smithsonian Institution Press.

Lamphere, Louise. 1974. "Women in Domestic Groups." In *Woman, Culture, & Society*, edited by Michelle Zimbalist Rosaldo and Louise Lamphere, pp. 97–112. Stanford, CA: Stanford University Press.

_____. 1995. "Feminist Anthropology: the Legacy of Elsie Clews Parsons." In *Women Writing Culture*, edited by Ruth Behar and Deborah Gordon, pp. 85–103. Berkeley: University of California Press.

_____. 1997. "The Domestic Sphere of Women and the Public World of Men: the Strengths and Limitations of an Anthropological Dichotomy." In *Gender in Cross-Cultural Perspective* (2nd ed.), edited by Caroline Brettell and Carolyn Sargent, pp. 82–91. Englewood Cliffs, NJ: Prentice Hall.

Landsman, Gail. 1995. "Negotiating Work and Womanhood." *American Anthropologist* 97 (1):33–40.

Leacock, Eleanor, ed. 1972. "Introduction." In *The Origin of the Family, Private*

Property and the State, by F. Engels. New York: International Publishers.
_____. 1978. "Women's Status in Egalitarian Society: Implications for Social Evolution." *Current Anthropology* 19 (2):247–75.

Leibowitz, Lila. 1983. "Origins of the Sexual Division of Labor." In *Women's Nature*, edited by M. Lowe and R. Hubbard, pp. 123–47. New York: Pergamon.

Lévi-Strauss, Claude. 1969. *The Elementary Structures of Kinship*. Boston: Beacon Press.

_____. 1971. "The Family." In *Man, Culture and Society*, edited by H. Shapiro. London: Oxford University Press.

Lewin, Ellen. 1990. "Claims to Motherhood: Custody Disputes and Maternal Strategies." In *Uncertain Terms: Negotiating Gender in American Culture*, edited by Faye Ginsburg and Anna L. Tsing, pp. 199–214. Boston: Beacon Press.

_____. 1993. *Lesbian Mothers: Accounts of Gender in American Culture*. Ithaca, NY: Cornell Univeristy Press.

Lewin, Tamar. 1998. "U.S. Colleges Begin to Ask, Where Have the Men Gone." *New York Times* CXLVIII (51,363): 1 and 28, December 6.

Lovejoy, C. Owen. 1981. "The Origins of Man." In *Science* 211:341–50.

Lugones, Maria, and Elizabeth Spelman. 1983. "Have We Got a Theory for You! Feminist Theory, Cultural Imperialism, and the Demand for 'The Woman's Voice.'" *Women's Studies International Forum* 6 (6):573–81.

Lutkehaus, Nancy. 1995. "Margaret Mead and the 'Rustling-of-the-Winds-in-the-Palm-Trees School' of Ethnography." In *Women Writing Culture*, edited by Ruth Behar and Deborah Gordon, pp. 186–206. Berkeley: University of California Press.

Maccoby, Eleanor. 1998. *The Two Sexes: Growing Up Apart, Coming Together*. Cambridge, MA: Belknap Pess.

Maccoby, Eleanor and Carol Jacklin. 1974. *The Psychology of Sex Differences*. Stanford, CA: Stanford University Press.

MacCormack, Carol. 1980. "Nature, Gender, and Culture: A Critique." In *Nature, Culture and Gender*, edited by Carol MacCormack and Marilyn Strathern, pp. 1–24. Cambridge: Cambridge University Press.

MacCormack, Carol, and Marilyn Strathern. 1980. *Nature, Culture and Gender*. Cambridge: Cambridge University Press.

Manson, W. C. 1986. "Sexual Cyclicity and Concealed Ovulation." *Journal of Human Evolution* 15:21–30.

Martin, Emily. 1987. *The Woman in the Body: A Cultural Analysis of Reproduction*. Boston: Beacon Press.

Martin, Kay and Barbara Voorhies. 1975. *Female of the Species*. New York: Columbia University Press.

Marx, Karl. 1992. *A Critique of Political Economy*, translated by Ben Fowles. New York: Penguin.

Marx, Karl, and Friedrich Engels. [1848] 1967. *The Communist Manifesto*. London: Penguin.

Mascia-Lees, Frances E., John Relethford, and Tom Sorger. 1986. "Evolutionary Perspectives on Permanent Breast Enlargement in Human Females." *American Anthropologist* 88 (2):423–28.

Mascia-Lees, Frances E. and Patricia Sharpe. 1992. "The Marked and the

Un(re)marked: Tattoo and Gender in Theory and Narrative." In *Tattoo, Torture, Mutilation and Adornment: The Denaturalization of the Body in Culture in Text*, edited by Frances E. Mascia-Lees and Patricia Sharpe, pp.145–69. New York: SUNY Press.

_____. 1994. "The Anthropological Unconscious." *American Anthropologist* 93 (3):649–60.

Mascia-Lees, Frances E., Patricia Sharpe, and Colleen B. Cohen. 1989. "The Post-Modernist Turn in Anthropology: Cautions from a Feminist Perspective." *Signs* 15 (1):7–33.

Mascia-Lees, Frances E., F. Tierson, and J. Relethford. 1989. "Investigating the Biocultural Dimensions of Human Sexual Behavior." *Medical Anthropology* 11(4):367–84.

Matthiasson, C. 1974. "Introduction." In *Sex Roles in Changing Cultures, Occasional Papers in Anthropology*, edited by A. McElroy and C. Matthiasson. New York: SUNY Buffalo Press.

McClaurin, Irma. 1996. *Women of Belize: Gender and Change in Central America*. Piscataway, NJ: Rutgers University Press.

McGee, R. Jon, and Richard L. Warms. 1996. *Anthropological Theory: An Introductory History*. Mountain View, CA: Mayfield.

Mead, Margaret. [1928] 1949. *Coming of Age in Samoa*. New York: Mentor Books.

_____. 1935. *Sex and Temperament in Three Primitive Societies*. New York: William Morrow.

Mernissi, Fatima. 1987. *Beyond the Veil: Male-Female Dynamics in a Modern Moslem Society*. Bloomington: Indiana University Press.

Meuller, M. 1977. "Women and Men: Power and Powerlessness in Lesotho." In *Women and National Development: The Complexities of Change*, edited by the Wellesley Editorial Committee, pp. 154–66. Chicago: University of Chicago Press.

Miller, James. 1993. *The Passion of Michel Foucault*. New York: Simon and Schuster.

Mohanty, Chandra Talpade, Ann Russo and Lourdes Torres, eds. 1991. *Third World Women and the Politics of Feminism*. Bloomington: Indiana University Press.

Moore, Henrietta. 1986. *Space, Text, and Gender: An Anthropological Study of the Marakwet of Kenya*. Cambridge: Cambridge University Press.

Moore, Robert. 1988. "Racist Stereotyping in the English Language." In *Racism and Sexism in America: An Integrated Study*, edited by Paula S. Rothenberg, pp 269–79. New York: St. Martin's.

Morbeck, Mary, Alsion Galloway, and Adrienne Zihlman, eds. 1997. *The Evolving Female: A Life-History Perspective*. Princeton, NJ: Princeton University Press.

Morgan, Lewis Henry. [1877] 1985. *Ancient Society*. Tucson: University of Arizona Press.

Morpeth, R., and P. Langton. 1973. "Contemporary Matriarchies, Women Alone: Independent or Complete." *Cambridge Anthropology* 1 (3):20–38.

Morris, Rosalind. 1994. "Three Sexes and Four Sexualities: Redressing the Discourses on Gender and Sexuality in Contemporary Thailand." *Positions* 2:15–43.

Murphy, Robert. 1971. *The Dialectics of Social Life*. New York: Basic Books.

Murphy, Yolanda, and Robert Murphy. 1974. *Women of the Forest*. New York: Columbia University Press.

Nanda, Serena. 1990. *Neither Male nor Female: The Hijras of India*. Belmont, CA: Wadsworth.

Nash, June, and Helen Safa, eds. 1980. *Sex and Class in Latin America: Women's Perspectives on Politics, Economics, and the Family in the Third World*. Westport, CT: Bergin and Garvey.

Nelkin, Dorothy, and M. Susan Lindee. 1995. *The DNA Mystique: The Gene as a Cultural Icon*. New York: W. H. Freeman.

Nelson, Sarah. 1997. "Diversity of the Upper Paleolithic 'Venus' Figurines and Archeological Mythology." In *Gender in Cross-Cultural Perspective* (2nd ed.), edited by Caroline Brettell and Carolyn Sargent, pp. 67–73. Englewood Cliffs, NJ: Prentice Hall.

Newsweek. January 30, 1995, p. 17.

Nielsen, Joyce M. 1990. *Sex and Gender in Society: Perspectives on Stratification* (2nd ed.). Prospect Heights, IL: Waveland Press.

Oboler, Regina Smith. 1993. "Is the Female Husband a Man? Woman/Woman Marriage Among the Nandi of Kenya." In *Talking About People*, edited by William Haviland and Robert Gordon, pp. 136–45. Mountain View, CA: Mayfield.

Ong, Aihwa. 1987. *Spirits of Resistance and Capitalist Discipline: Factory Women in Malaysia*. Albany: SUNY Press.

Ortner, Sherry. 1974. "Is Female to Male as Nature is to Culture"? In *Woman, Culture, & Society*, edited by Michelle Zimbalist Rosaldo and Louise Lamphere, pp. 67–88. Stanford, CA: Stanford University Press.

———. 1984. "Theory in Anthropology since the Sixties." *Society for Comparative Studies in Society and History* 26 (1):126–65.

———. 1996. *Making Gender: The Politics and Erotics of Culture*. Boston: Beacon Press.

Ortner, Sherry, and Harriet Whitehead, eds. 1981. *Sexual Meanings: The Cultural Construction Gender and Sexuality*. Cambridge: Cambridge University Press.

Peletz, Michael. 1996. *Reason and Passion: Representations of Gender in Malay Society*. Berkeley: University of California Press.

Pratt, Mary Louise. 1986. "Fieldwork in Common Places." In *Writing Culture: The Poetics and Politics of Ethnography*, edited by James Clifford and George Marcus, pp. 27–50. Berkeley: University of California Press.

Quinn, Naomi. 1977. "Anthropological Studies of Women's Status." *Annual Review of Anthropology* 6:181–225.

Rapp, Rayna. 1990. "Constructing Amniocentesis: Maternal and Medical Discourses." In *Uncertain Terms: Negotiating Gender in American Culture*, edited by Faye Ginsburg and Anna L. Tsing, pp. 28–42. Boston: Beacon Press.

Reiter, Rayna R., ed. 1975a. *Toward an Anthropology of Women*. New York: Monthly Review.

———. 1975b. "Introduction." In *Toward an Anthropology of Women*, edited by Rayna R. Reiter, pp. 11–19. New York: Monthly Review.

———. 1975c. "Men and Women in the South of France." In *Toward an Anthropology of Women*, edited by Rayna R. Reiter, pp. 252–82. New York: Monthly Review.

Rosaldo, Michelle Zimbalist, 1974. "Woman, Culture, & Society: A Theoretical Overview." In *Woman, Culture, & Society*, edited by Michelle Zimbalist Rosaldo and Louise Lamphere, pp. 17–42. Stanford, CA: Stanford University Press.

Rosaldo, Michelle Zimbalist, and Louise Lamphere, eds. 1974. *Woman, Culture, & Society*. Stanford, CA: Stanford University Press.

Rosaldo, Renato. 1989. *Culture and Truth: The Remaking of Social Analysis*. Boston: Beacon Press.

Rowell, T. 1972. "Female Reproductive Cycles and Social Behavior in Primates." *Advances in the Study of Behavior* 4:69–105.

Rubin, Gayle. 1975. "The Traffic in Women: Notes on the 'Political Economy' of Sex." In *Toward an Anthropology of Women*, edited by Rayna R. Reiter, pp. 157–210. New York: Monthly Review.

Sacks, Karen. 1974. "Engels Revisited: Women, The Organization of Production and Private Property." In *Woman, Culture, & Society*, edited by Michelle Zimbalist Rosaldo and Louise Lamphere, pp. 207–22. Stanford, CA: Stanford University Press.

_____. 1979. *Sisters and Wives*.Westport, CT: Greenwood.

Said, Edward. 1979. *Orientalism*. New York: Random House.

Sanday, Peggy. 1981. *Female Power and Male Dominance: On the Origins of Sexual Inequality*. Cambridge: Cambridge University Press.

Scheper-Hughes, Nancy. 1995. "The Primacy of the Ethical: Propositions for a Militant Anthropology." *Current Anthropology* 36 (3):409–20.

Schlegel, Alice. 1972. *Male Dominance and Female Autonomy*. New Haven: HRAF.

_____. 1977. *Sexual Stratification: A Cross-Cultural View*. New York: Columbia University Press.

Science Digest. 1982. (July):64–65.

Shostak, Marjorie. 1983. *Nisa: The Life and Words of a !Kung Woman*. New York: Vintage.

Slocum, Sally. 1975. "Woman the Gatherer: Male Bias in Anthropology." In *Toward an Anthropology of Women*, edited by Rayna R. Reiter, pp. 36–50. New York: Monthly Review.

Smith, Sheldon, and Philip Young. 1998. *Cultural Anthropology*. Boston: Allyn and Bacon.

Smuts, Barbara. 1985. *Sex and Friendship in Baboons*. New York: Aldine.

Spencer, Herbert. 1884. *The Study of Sociology*. New York: D. Appleton.

Spender, Dale. 1980. *Man Made Language*. London: Routledge.

Spivak, Gayatri Chakravorty. 1990. "The Intervention Interview." *The Post-Colonial Critique: Interviews, Strategies, Dialogues*, edited by Sarah Harasym. London: Routledge.

Stacey, Judith. 1988. "Can there be a Feminist Ethnography?" *Women's Studies International Forum* 11 (1):21–27.

Stack, Carol. 1974. "Sex Roles and Survival Strategies in an Urban Black Community." In *Woman, Culture, & Society*, edited by Michelle Zimbalist Rosaldo and Louise Lamphere, pp. 113–28. Stanford, CA: Stanford University Press.

Stewart, Kathleen C. 1990. "Backtalking the Wilderness: 'Appalachian' Engenderings." In *Uncertain Terms: Negotiating Gender in American Culture*, edited by Faye Ginsburg and Anna L. Tsing, pp. 43–56. Boston: Beacon Press.

Stocking, George W. 1987. *Victorian Anthropology*. New York: The Free Press.

Stoler, Ann. 1977. "Class Structure and Female Authority in Rural Java." *Signs* 3:74–89.

Stoller, Paul. 1997. *Sensuous Scholarship*. Philadelphia: University of Pennsylvania Press.

Strathern, Marilyn. 1972. *Women in Between: Female Roles in a Male World: Mount Hagen, New Guinea*. London: Seminar Press.

Strauss, Claudia, and Naomi Quinn. 1997. *A Cognitive Theory of Cultural Meaning*. Cambridge: Cambridge University Press.

Tannen, Deborah. 1987. *That's Not What I Meant! How Conversational Style Makes or Breaks Relationships*. New York: Ballantine.

Tanner, Nancy. 1981. *On Becoming Human*. Cambridge: Cambridge University Press.

Tanner, Nancy and Adrienne Zilhman. 1976. "Women in Evolution. Part I: Innovation and Selection in Human Origins." *Signs* 3 (1):585–608.

Thomson, Rosemarie Garland. 1996. "Introduction." In *Freakery: Cultural Spectacles of the Extraordinary Body*, edited by Rosemarie Garland Thomson, pp. 1–19. New York: NYU Press.

Trinh, T. Minh-ha. 1989. *Women, Native, Other*. Bloomington: Indiana University Press.

Tsing, Anna L. 1993. *In the Realm of the Diamond Queen*. New Jersey: Princeton University Press.

Tylor, Edward B. 1871. *Primitive Culture: Researches into the Development of Mythology, Philosophy, Religion, Language, Art, and Custom*. 2 vols. London: J. Murray.

Villapando, Venny. 1989. "Mail Order Brides." In *Making Waves: An Anthology of Writing by and about Asian-American Women*, edited by Diana Yen-Mei Wong and Emilya Cachapero, pp. 318–26. Boston: Beacon Press.

Washburn, Sherwood, and C. Lancaster. 1968. "The Evolution of Hunting." In *Man the Hunter*, edited by R. B. Lee and Irven DeVore, pp. 293–303. Chicago: Aldine Press.

Webster, Paula. 1975. "Matriarchy: A Vision of Power." In *Toward an Anthropology of Women*, edited by Rayna R. Reiter, pp. 141–56. New York: Monthly Review.

Weiner, Annette. 1979. *Women of Value, Men of Renown*. Austin: University of Texas Press.

Whiting, B., and J. Whiting. 1975. *Children of Six Cultures: A Psycho-Cultural Analysis*. Cambridge: Harvard University Press.

Whyte, Martin K. 1978. *The Status of Women in Preindustrial Societies*. Princeton, NJ: Princeton University Press.

Wilson, Edward O. 1975. *Sociobiology: The New Synthesis*. Cambridge: Harvard University Press.

Wolf, Margery. 1972. *Women and the Family in Rural Taiwan*. Stanford, CA: Stanford University Press.

Wolf, Naomi. 1992. *The Beauty Myth*. New York: Anchor.

Wood, J. 1982. "Models of Human Evolution." *Science* 217:296–97.

Wright, Robert. 1994. *The Moral Animal: Evolutionary Psychology and Everyday*

Life. New York: Vintage.
Yanagisako, Sylvia. 1977. "Women-Centered Kin Networks in Urban Bilateral Kinship." *American Ethnologist* 2:207–26.

Index